THEORIES OF
MORAL DEVELOPMENT

THEORIES OF
MORAL DEVELOPMENT

By

JOHN MARTIN RICH, Ph.D.

The University of Texas at Austin

JOSEPH L. DeVITIS, Ph.D.

The University of Tennessee at Martin

CHARLES C THOMAS • PUBLISHER
Springfield • Illinois • U.S.A.

Published and Distributed Throughout the World by

CHARLES C THOMAS • PUBLISHER
2600 South First Street
Springfield, Illinois 62717

© *1985 by* CHARLES C THOMAS • PUBLISHER

ISBN 0-398-05092-9

Library of Congress Catalog Card Number: 84-16345

Printed in the United States of America
Q-R-3

Library of Congress Cataloging in Publication Data

Rich, John Martin
   Theories of moral development.

   Bibliography: p.
   Includes index.
   1. Moral development. 2. Developmental psychology.
3. Educational psychology. I. DeVitis, Joseph L.
II. Title.
BF723.M54R53 1985   155.2'5'   84-16345
ISBN 0-398-05092-9

PREFACE AND ACKNOWLEDGMENTS

THIS book represents the authors' conviction that interpretive, normative, and critical perspectives be brought to bear in the analysis of moral development theory. From the book's inception, the purpose has been to set the stage for an introductory meeting ground that might engage those who are interested in reconciling the separate paths often taken by students in psychology, education, philosophy, and social criticism. Thus the objective is to bring together these divergent strands in moral development theory; as a consequence, thinkers whose contributions to moral development theory have been neglected are accorded more complete treatment.

We have profited by the reactions of students and colleagues to the book's conceptual framework. We wish to thank Arthur W. Chickering of the Center for Higher Education at Memphis State University for his gracious and helpful review of the manuscript's prospectus, Betty A. Sichel of C.W. Post Center, Long Island University, for her supportive correspondence and collegial advice, Payne E.L. Thomas of Charles C Thomas, Publisher for his encouragement and conviction of the project's merit, The University of Tennessee at Martin for providing a research grant which aided the project's completion, and Michael Fadus for his efficient typing. Those debts may be compensated if this effort asssists readers to better appreciate the meaning behind William James's apt characterization of "good education": namely, to be able to recognize good men and women when we see them.

CONTENTS

Page

Preface and Acknowledgements v

Chapter

1. MORAL DEVELOPMENT IN EDUCATION AND PSYCHOLOGY:
   AN OVERVIEW 3
   A Look Ahead.. 4
   Key Terms... 5
   Individual Autonomy and Social Stability 8
   Durkheim's Paradigm 11
2. MORAL DEVELOPMENT IN CHILDHOOD..................... 17
   Freud: Enlightened Self-Interest 17
   Adler: Social Interest 24
   Jung: From Fantasy to Reality 33
   Sears: Behavioral Child Rearing........................ 42
   Piaget: Cognitive Moral Judgment...................... 46
3. MORAL DEVELOPMENT IN ADOLESCENCE 53
   Havighurst: Developmental Tasks 53
   Erikson: Identity Crisis and Ideology.................... 59
4. MORAL DEVELOPMENT AND HIGHER EDUCATION 66
   Jacob: Value Change and Curriculum 66
   Chickering: Education and Integrity 69
   Perry and Heath: Growth, Commitment, and Maturity 74
   Keniston: Uncommitted and Dissident Youth 83

5. MORAL DEVELOPMENT THROUGH THE
    LIFE SPAN 87
    Kohlberg: Cognitive Moral Development Theory 87
    Levinson: The Seasons of Adult Life Cycles 98
    Fowler: Faith and Human Development 105
    Loevinger: Milestones of Ego Development 111
    Gilligan: In a Different Voice 117
Index 121

THEORIES OF
MORAL DEVELOPMENT

CHAPTER ONE

MORAL DEVELOPMENT IN EDUCATION AND PSYCHOLOGY: AN OVERVIEW

MORAL development was cited as a primary responsibility for public schools by more than two-thirds of the respondents to the 1975 and 1976 Gallup polls on education. At the same time, psychologists and other mental health practitioners have been perplexed about what constitutes "moral development" and how descriptions and explanations of it can contribute to a harmonizing of individual needs and societal pressures. Recent crises, from the civil rights movement in the 1960's through issues raised by the Moral Majority today, have served to muddle in the public mind such distinctions as morals, manners, mores, and ethics. Belief systems do not clarify what is actually entailed in moral decision and "moral development." That is to say, popular crises in morality have tended to divert energies away from more critical and fundamental inquiry into human nature, both human capabilities and limitations. Any fair assessment of moral accountability requires that the human being be capable of doing that for which he is judged.

It is for this reason that scholars and practitioners need to retrieve, elucidate, and analyze critically those systematic, theoretical syntheses of moral development that are already available and to evaluate whether these alternatives offer a way out of current confusion about moral decision making. By becoming clearer about foundational bases for morality, both the professional educator and mental health practitioner will be able to achieve a firmer grasp, or conceptual handle, on those issues which seem to be so important, but con-

3

fusing, to the lay public. As theories of moral development provide new insights, opportunities improve for the discovery of new ideas about morality. This is more the case when a consensual body of knowledge about moral development is made available to both lay and professional audiences so that they can engage in dialogue.

Most textbooks limit themselves to certain major models of moral development, especially the cognitive-structural psychology of Piaget and Kohlberg. While this is an important approach and will be treated herein, what is missing is a more comprehensive treatment of competing theories. Thus this book affords a comprehensive treatment and elaboration of *competing options* in moral development as generated by a host of other psychological theories. It therefore relates different universes of discourse about moral development so that professionals and laypersons alike will be able to articulate and refine moral issues out of *diverse* frameworks.

A LOOK AHEAD

The introductory chapter clarifies key terms and lays the background from which theories of moral development and education have been formulated as a response to the question of the essential competing demands for individual autonomy and social stability. Since Emile Durkheim focuses so clearly on that question and because so many subsequent developmental theorists either build upon or attempt to move around his theories, Durkheim's sociological paradigm will serve as a base for further discussion.

Chapter Two will survey competing models from various schools of thought on the initial origins of morality in childhood: Freud's psychoanalytical model; Alfred Adler's views from Individual Psychology; Jung's neo-analytical contributions; Robert Sears' behavioral theory; and Piaget's very influential cognitive-structural approach.

Chapter Three includes Erik H. Erikson's socio-cultural synthesis, particularly the problem of "identity" crisis; and Robert J. Havighurst's description of "developmental tasks," which seem to be especially relevant to adolescent life adjustment.

Chapter Four covers the explicit body of data-based research that has focused on the recent knowledge explosion about how higher education either affects or does not affect moral development. Surveyed here will be such diverse thinkers as Arthur Chickering (Vectors of Development); William Perry (theory of intellectual and ethical development); Douglas Heath (model of maturing); Roy Heath (personality typologies); and Kenneth Keniston (on student radicals and the alienated and uncommitted).

Chapter Five presents a panoramic view, drawn from multiple sources, of life-long patterns and detours (some presumably invariant, others presumably changeable) that stem from another and recent and still growing body of research investigation. Included here are Lawrence Kohlberg's dominant paradigm of a universal, hierarchical form of moral development; Carol Gilligan's counter-paradigm of women's moral growth in particular social contexts which vary through life's changing circumstances; Jane Loevinger's "milestones of development," which adapts ego-psychology to different life stages; Daniel Levinson's more specific findings on the "seasons of a man's life," that focus on adult problems of work, love, security, and needs for continuous reassessment and enrichment; and James Fowler's studies of faith and development in the life cycle. As life expectancy increases and social roles and expectations change (and leisure becomes more fashionable and problematic), life-span moral development is fast becoming a crucial issue in the daily existence of ordinary people.

Accordingly, this book will attempt to promote avenues for a common civic education about morality and at the same time encourage a morality of tolerance about those many concerns which appear to be unquenchable and problematic. In this sense, it will have better prepared its readers to be interpretive, normative, and critical analysts who also recognize the possibilities of error and imponderables.

KEY TERMS

Certain key terms which may appear frequently should be clarified. Whenever a thinker coins his own definition that is at odds with those presented below, then this stipulative definition will be indicated at the appropriate point.

Morality, first of all, should be distinguished from manners and mores. *Manners* are concerned with matters of taste and etiquette based on prudential judgments. Such judgments concern circumspection, shrewdness, or wiseness in judgments about practical affairs. Although one's prudential judgments and moral judgments will occasionally coincide, they frequently may differ. One may decide to do something because it will help one to advance, gain control over something or someone, or for financial gain even though the morality of the act may be questionable. Telling the truth may be the moral thing to do, but to do so may impede one's professional advancement in a certain situation; therefore, the individual may find it prudent to distort, be evasive, or lie.

By *mores* is meant the fixed morally-binding customs of a particular group. Mores vary considerably cross-culturally and throughout human history, ranging from the noblest behavior to the approval of slavery, infanticide, burning infidels at the stake, genocide, and other practices.

In contrast, *morality* is a system of conduct based on moral principles. That which is *moral*, therefore, relates to principles of right conduct in behavior; the behavior complies with accepted principles of what is considered right, virtuous or just. To say that a certain act is immoral means that it is unvirtuous or contrary to morality because it does not conform to principles of right conduct.

Two cognate terms should be considered: *amoral* and *nonmoral*. Amoral has more than one meaning insofar as it may refer to someone who is indifferent to or does not care to abide by moral codes. Or it may refer to someone who lacks moral sensibility, such as infants, because of immaturity. It may also be equated with nonmoral, an act which is neither moral nor immoral, such as a decision to buy a particular tie.

The study of the nature of morality consists of two major approaches: the scientific and the philosophical. The scientific utilizes social and behavioral science methodology to uncover how people actually behave and what they believe about morality. The philosophical approach, in contrast, is known as *ethics*, which is a study of the nature of morality and moral acts. Ethics is divided into normative ethics and metaethics. Normative ethics is concerned with what people ought to do (Should one always tell the truth?) and with systems of ethics (Epicureanism, Stoicism, Kantianism, utilitarianism, etc.). Metaethics analyzes ethical language and the justification of ethical inquiry and judgments.

The term, *development*, refers to progressive and continuous changes in the organism from birth to death. These changes can include changes in the shape and integration of bodily parts into functional parts; and intellectual, social, emotional, or moral development that may occur at different periods of an individual's life. These periods can be conveniently divided into infancy, childhood, adolescence, young adulthood, middle age, and old age (however, different theories may divide or combine them differently).

Development can be ascribed to the interaction of the organism and the environment in which both learned behavior and heredity are operative. Though heredity may include physical characteristics (hair and eye color, hair distribution, etc.), maturation is of greater interest in developmental studies. By *maturation* is meant that part of the development process that can be attributed to heredity or is species-specific behavior, such as walking.

Moral development refers to growth of the individual's ability to distinguish right from wrong, to develop a system of ethical values, and to learn to act morally. A moral development theory explains how individuals develop morally. A *theory* is a body of principles used to explain phenomena. Related is the term *moral education*, which refers to instruction in moral rules of conduct for the purpose of developing good character traits and ethical behavior. Such instruction may be systematically planned (as with moral education programs in churches and schools) or unplanned (as a parent reprimanding her offspring for immoral behavior).

The process of socialization and education should be distinguished because moral development occurs not only through maturation and education but socialization as well. *Socialization* is the process by which an individual acquires the knowledge, skills, and behavior that will make him or her an adequate member of society.

In contrast, *education* is a generic term that refers to an intentional process that has objectives, content, and outcomes and takes place both in educational institutions and informal settings. Education is designed not only to transmit knowledge and the cultural heritage but to improve individuals by engaging their thinking, feeling, and action. Objectives refer to what one hopes to achieve in the process; the content is what is taught, and the outcomes are what is actually achieved. That objectives are stipulated shows that the process is intentional and pre-planned, not accidental or inadvertent (as in the case of some learning).

What is the difference, then, between socialization and education? One of the chief tasks of socialization is the learning of roles (son, daughter, friend, student, and so on). Thus, one learns appropriate roles for his age, sex, social class, and personal responsibilities. Socialization processes instill proper social rules and thereby help preserve social institutions. Though schools and other institutions and agencies engage in socialization, it is a primary activity of the family. Education, on the other hand, is usually designed to develop new ideas and improve society by providing students with requisite knowledge and reflective abilities. This is less true in the early grades in which the acquisition of basic skills and a rudimentary knowledge of the cultural heritage are emphasized.

INDIVIDUAL AUTONOMY AND SOCIAL STABILITY

Societies are interested in maintaining themselves over extended time periods and preserving their cultural heritage. At the same time, most societies seek to improve themselves — promote greater economic growth, advancements in technology, better international relations, higher educational standards, or in some other way. Certain forms of independence and autonomy are needed among citizens to enjoy the creativity to effect these improvements. Not all changes, however, are improvements or reforms, and some reforms may threaten older values and traditions. Thus, a tension arises between individual autonomy and social stability.

One explanation for how stability is maintained in society is based on a social disorganization theory.[1] A social system is organized through a consistent set of norms and values that fosters orderly and predictable social action among its members. Leaders of society try to foster a normative consensus. Social disorganization results whenever orderly social interaction breaks down and normative consensus fails to be achieved. Disorganization stems from anomie (a state of normlessness) or a lack of consensus on norms. Whenever disorganization and anomie occur, deviant behavior is likely to result; and as disorganization grows, deviance and violence increase. Social disorganization is expressed in inadequate institutionalization of goals, inappropriate procedures for achieving goals, weakened social control, and shifting population.

Thus the tasks for avoiding social disorganization are to create a normative consensus, to develop compelling goals and consistent procedures for achieving them, and to institute effective socialization practices.

Each individual who strives for independence will not likely become independent without developing certain skills and competencies that are created within various authority patterns. In other words, the authority of the home and school become models for the meaning of one's search for independence. The process of becoming independent also involves assuming some of the different authority types for oneself, to become increasingly one's own authority and, as a young adult's new responsibilities should call for it (as when one becomes a parent or a teacher), to play the appropriate authority-type role to the young of the next generation.

Angyal has postulated an approach which involves two different but complementary orientations.[2] One is that the organism tends to strive for increased autonomy, even though there are heteronomous influences that decrease it. According to this theory, the life process is characterized by two components: autonomy and heteronomy, or self-government and government from outside.

---

[1]Examples of the social disorganization theory: Merton, Robert K.: *Social Theory and Social Structure*, Glencoe, Ill., Free Press, 1957; Cohen, Albert K., *Deviance and Control*. Englewood Cliffs, N.J., Prentice Hall, 1966; and McGee, Reece, *Social Disorganization in America*, San Francisco, Chandler, 1962.

[2]Angyal, Andras: *Neurosis and Treatment: A Holistic Approach*. New York, Wiley, 1965.

Angyal suggests that there can be not only a lack of autonomy (one of the characteristics of neurotic living) but an excess of autonomous striving. A lack of autonomy is manifested in excessive conformism, inability to form independent judgments or disagreee with anyone, and dependence upon others far in excess of necessity.

But less widely recognized is excessive autonomous striving. Here the characteristic behavior includes extreme resentment and rejection of the influence of others, intolerance and rebelliousness, and the need to test continually or "prove" oneself by acts designed to show competency or mastery.[3] Excessive autonomous striving, frequently the pattern of adolescents and adults who are unsure of their mastery over their environment, should not be confused with healthy forms of autonomy.

Angyal calls the healthy form of heteronomy *homonomy.* "The person behaves as if he were seeking a place for himself in a larger unit of which he strives to become a part."[4] One cannot master the environment by force or violence, but must understand and comply with environmental laws, which is to adopt a homonomous attitude. Thus autonomy and homonomy, for Angyal, are complementary orientations that have their norms in healthy expression.

These complementary orientations can also be found in Riesman's interpretation of the autonomous person as one who is capable of conforming to societal norms but free to choose whether or not to conform; he is less the creature of circumstance than other characterological types, such as "tradition-directed," "inner-directed," and "other-directed" persons.[5]

Thus the choices in human development, for Angyal and Riesman, are to seek complementary orientations, or to emphasize either autonomy or social stabililty. Stability would be maintained by adopting a homonomous attitude and instituting other measures (mentioned above) to avert social disorganization. Whereas for autonomy, "the individual increasingly comes to feel," according to

[3]Ibid., p. 12.
[4]Ibid., p. 15.
[5]Riesman, D., Glazer, N., and Denney, R.: *The Lonely Crowd.* New Haven, Yale, 1952.

Rogers, "that the locus of evaluation lies within himself."[6] Other choices, in addition to those previously stated, will be developed in subsequent chapters.

DURKHEIM'S PARADIGM

Perhaps the most classic attempt to weigh the seemingly competing interests of social stability and individual autonomy can be found in the pioneering work of the French sociologist Emile Durkheim (1858-1916). Indeed, his seminal effort to articulate these alternative claims builds a basis for analysis in moral development which later theorists would have to attack head on, or at least acknowledge, in their own attempts to construct "better bridges" for ethical argumentation. Unfortunately, Durkheim has not received the wide attention that he deserves. For that reason, and for the purpose of clarifying subsequent models of moral development, Durkheim's original paradigm will be analyzed and discussed in some detail.

According to Durkheim, there are three basic elements in the internalization of moral values: (1) "the spirit of authority and discipline"; (2) "attachment to social groups"; and (3) "autonomy," or self-determination.

Durkheim speaks of authority and discipline as moral imperatives which "perform an important function in forming character and personality in general."[7] He posits authority and discipline as essential because of their capacity for restraint, allowing sentient human beings to "contain our passions, our desires, our habits, and subject them to law."[8] Thus, without discipline, man would be a slave to impulse and, as a consequence, be neither free nor happy. At the same time, discipline promotes its own self-regulating patterns of conduct and cooperation which make for a kind of "social

---

[6]Rogers, Carl.: *On Becoming a Person.* Boston: Houghton Mifflin, 1961, p. 119.
[7]Durkheim, Emile: *Moral Education: A Study in the Theory and Application of the Sociology of Knowledge* (1925), Everett K. Wilson and Herman Schnurer (Tr.). New York, Free Press, 1961, p. 46.
[8]*Ibid.*

glue" without which human organization would be impossible. Taken together, then, authority and discipline permit us to safeguard social stability and to establish possibilites for individual autonomy. For Durkheim, moral rules and human liberties are not viewed as exclusive or antithetical terms, but as part of concrete social practice and specific social context.

Pedagogically, it becomes the function of the educator to inculcate those habits of conduct, those norms and rules, which serve to integrate the child into the stable, ongoing rhythms of social reality. Indeed, Durkheim implies that discipline itself is a moral end in that it mediates the child's initial egoism.

In this regard, some observers have accused Durkheim of failing to distinguish "socialization" from "education."[9] Simply given his emphasis on authority and discipline, socialization would appear to be Durkheim's chief intention. However, as will be pointed out subsequently, he was also vitally interested in education *qua* education.

The second main feature of Durkheim's moral paradigm lies in the individual's attachment to the group. In his very first book, *The Division of Labor* (1893), Durkheim presages his allegiance to the social framework of all morality: "Let social life disappear and moral life will disappear with it, since it would no longer have any objective."[10] In large measure, Durkehim is also foreshadowing later social milieu theorists such as George Herbert Mead in his insistence on identifying the moral life as moving beyond the realm of the "I" to that of the "We." Like some of these subsequent thinkers, Durkheim couches his terms in an evolutionary context:

> Family, nation, and humanity represent different phases of our social and moral evolution, stages that prepare for, and build upon, one another . . . . Just as each has its part to play in historical development, they mutually complement each other in the present.[11]

---

[9]"Socialization" can be viewed as "the process by which an individual acquires the knowledge, skills, and behavior that will make him an adequate member of society . . . . One of the chief tasks in socialization is the learning of roles . . . . Socialization processes instill proper social rules and thereby help preserve social institutions. Education, on the other hand, is usually designed to change and improve individuals and society by providing requisite knowledge and relfective abilities." Rich, John Martin: *Discipline and Authority in School and Family*. Lexington, Lexington Books, 1982, pp. 115, 134.

[10]Durkehim, Emile: *The Division of Labor* (1893), George Simpson (Tr.). New York, Macmillan, 1933, p. 399.

[11]*Ibid.*

During Durkheim's lifetime, the contemporary milieu in France and other Western societies exhibited tendencies toward normlessness or a lack of fixedness in moral authority (what Durkheim terms "anomie"), precarious signposts of imbalance in social attachment. These imbalances are symptomatic of what Durkheim calls "excessive individualism" or "excessive integration," both of which result, he claims, in abnormal increases in suicide:[12]

> Both suicidal types are defined in terms of *attachment* to collectively shared moral concepts, egoistic suicide being due to insufficient attachment to shared moral beliefs and altruistic suicide being the result of excessive solidarity with, and devotion to, group ends.[13]

Durkheim's classic study of suicide casts in bold relief the need to balance social stability with growth in individual autonomy if humankind is to survive and overcome conditions of personal and institutional disorganization.

The third component in Durkheim's moral paradigm, autonomy and self-determination, shows most clearly how he weds the competing demands for solidarity and individuality. According to most modern ethical theories, especially since Immanuel Kant, action and behavior cannot be judged "moral" unless it is accompanied by some substantial degree of "autonomous" reflection on the part of the moral actor. That is to say, the moral agent must be aware of, and understand, those rules of conduct which surround his/her moral decision making. It is for this reason that Durkheim attempts to liberate man from "direct dependence on things" by a form of concerted, rational, and scientific investigation of the external data around him:

> We fashion [autonomy] . . . ourselves to the extent that we achieve a more complete knowledge of things. [Autonomy] does not imply that the human being, in any of his aspects, escapes the world and its laws . . . . But, if in some measure we are the products of things, we can, through science, use our understanding to control both the things that exert an influence upon us and this influence itself. In this way, we again become our master.[14]

---

[12]Durkheim, Emile: *Suicide: A Study in Sociology* (1897), J.A. Spaulding and George Simpson (Tr.). New York, Free Press, 1952.
[13]Wellwork, Ernest: *Durkheim: Morality and Milieu*. Cambridge, Harvard U.P., 1972, pp. 48-49.
[14]Durkheim, Emile: *Moral Education*, pp. 114, 119.

Consequently, educators do not merely inculcate habits of conduct; they also instill in students an understanding of social reality which will enable them to shape their moral destiny. However, it should be noted once again that Durkheim never makes morality an entity unto itself or solely an instrument of individual human creation. Man's moral actions always derive from the social world: "It is a dangerous illusion to imagine that morality is a personal artifact; and that consequently we have it completely under our control."[15]

In a briefer section of his *Moral Education*, Durkheim traces several models of personality which resemble some modern prototypes in the literature of social and psychological theory. He postulates that these models are representative of "two extreme and opposed types in men's moral character." The first, more dominant, type he characterizes as being "sensitive to the rule," i.e., those persons in society who are predisposed to authority and discipline. This moral personality is happiest when duty, couched in rationality, can be executed properly (Durkheim cites the philosopher Kant as a prototypal example). The second personality type is more apt to be recognizable for its propensity to "spend" itself by an "outward expansiveness." More bound by the emotions, these individuals like to help others and do not act strictly by reason or logic. In this instance, Durkheim is already introducing a personality type which would later be described in various other terms by future psychologists and social theorists.[16]

Echoing Max Weber, Durkheim also speaks of "charismatic" figures who influence cold social facts and the inevitable movement of history. Socrates, Moses, Christ, Buddha, Mohammed, Martin Luther — all are illustrative of "great men" who have transcended, in substantial measure, existing social norms and more "deficient" codes of conduct.

Yet Durkheim's inclusion of the need for movers in history intimates, as an appendage, his own felt inner conflict in linking moral

---

[15]*Ibid.*

[16]For example, as someone imbued with "social interest" by Alfred Adler; as an "extrovert" by Carl Jung; and as an "other-directed" person by David Riesman. Similarly, Durkheim's "sensitive-to-the-rule" types seem to parallel Jung's "introverts" and Riesman's "inner-directed" figures. For Adler, such personalities might be viewed as "lacking in social interest."

logic so intimately with social logic. Indeed, the "science of morality" he has been seeking may rest on a subtle form of reductionism. Durkheim's almost mimetic identification with the social world forces his conception of morality into problematic corners. In the words of one critic, "It precludes the legitimacy of a morality more adequate than systems of values and ideals of societies past, present and future."[17]

There is an even graver, more dangerous, implication in Durkheim's theory of moral development:

> For example, it implies that the authority, the norms and rules and principles that defined, for instance, the Nazi moral system must be considered as legitimate as any others that have served to sustain the social fabric of a collectivity.[18]

On the other hand, more sympathetic interpreters cite passages in Durkheim's work in which he contends that "all human societies are not of equal value."[19]

Despite these differences in interpretation, it must be granted that Durkheim's dominant sense of relativism tends to nullify the possibility of universalizing moral principles within his own paradigm. It is this departure from traditional post-Kantian ethics which has perhaps drawn the most obvious and sizable criticism from modern scholars and may be the primary reason for their relative lack of interest in Durkheim's model of moral development.

Nevertheless, Durkheim's paradigm can be disregarded only with peril because it does highlight social facts and actual social practices and contexts in a way which contemporary theories, from the psychoanalytic school to cognitive-structural psychology, sometimes

[17]Prakash, Madhu Suri: Reflections on Durkheim's moral education. In Roemer, Robert E. (Ed.): *Philosophy of Education 1983: Proceedings of the Thirty-Ninth Annual Meeting of the Philosophy of Education Society*. Normal, Illinois State University, 1984, p. 344.

[18]*Ibid.* For more general treatments of Durkheim's analysis of moral development and education, see Lukes, Steven: *Emile Durkheim, His Life and Work: A Historical and Critical Study*. London, Allen Lane, 1973; Nisbet, Robert: *The Sociology of Emile Durkheim*. New York, Oxford U.P., 1974; and Gehlke, Charles E.: *Emile Durkheim's Contributions to Sociological Theory*. New York, AMS, 1968.

[19]Durkheim, Emile: *Moral Education*, p. 79.

seem to skim, gloss over, or neglect altogether.[20] Durkheim was among the earliest researchers to make us aware of the critical importance of social forces and how they influence our interpretation of morality. Moreover, his sociology of knowledge reminds us that morality is a matter of concrete action and behavior as well as mere abstract thought, i.e., that what one *does* may be as significant as what one says.[21]

Finally, Durkheim makes us face an often overlooked question which may be crucial to moral accountability and moral development: given the powerful impingements of one's culture, how and to what extent can men be properly asked to perform in a "moral" manner? At what point are we really asking them to do what might be morally impossible?

Subsequent theorists to be dealt with in this text may or may not have paid heed to Durkheim's contributions. And that may help explain, at least in part, why we are still grappling with roughly the same central issues which he described so precisely nearly a century ago.

---

[20]In this connection, Durkheim's views dovetail with those of Freud to the extent that the competing demands of individual versus social life posit an inevitable, often irreconcilable, tension throughout human history. Some other contemporary theorists, such as Piaget and Kohlberg, have taken Durkheim very seriously, indeed. A substantial part of Piaget's *The Moral Judgment of the Child*, dealt with in Chapter 2 of this text, is devoted to a critical revision of Durkheim's theses in *Moral Education*. Meanwhile, Kohlberg has traced moral development theory according to "post-Durkheimian" and "post-Piagetian" paradigms in his "The development of children's orientation toward a moral order," *Vita Humana*, 6:11, 1963.

[21]For a broad view of the entire "attitude/behavior" dichotomy in social science research, see Deutscher, Irwin: *What We Say/What We Do*. Glenview, Scott, Foresman, 1973.

CHAPTER TWO

MORAL DEVELOPMENT IN CHILDHOOD

FREUD: ENLIGHTENED SELF-INTEREST

PERHAPS the most significant, controversial theorist and thera-
pist in the relatively short history of psychology, Sigmund
Freud has enormously influenced personal and cultural judgments
since he strode upon the intellectual scene in late-nineteenth century
Austria. Theoretical constructions of personality, power, culture,
child-rearing practices, even historical and literary criticism, to
name only a few areas of discourse, were to be radically altered as a
result. Freud's psychoanalytic contributions to the dialogue on
morality are most germane to the developmental stages of early
childhood—those years on which he laid so much stress. Indeed, his
theory of morality, though more submerged, may be as important
and controversial as his more widely known views of psycho-sexual
development. Because of the magnitude of his impact, for good and/
or ill, Freud's notions on morality will be analyzed as they apply to
several major arenas of discussion and contention: (1) his overarching thesis of a "universal" paradigm which presumably governs all
morality; (2) his specific treatment of alleged differences in how men
and women develop; and (3) the ramifications and shortcomings of
his theory for future constructions of moral reality.

As a "depth" psychologist who "pried open" the primacy of sexuality and the unconscious in a relatively closed Victorian world, Freud
also carried on a battle similar to that waged by Durkheim in the sociological sphere. That is, Freud, like Durkheim, was interested

principally in balancing the often irreconcilable demands of individual versus social life. Given his own theoretical constructs, Freud admits that the task of morality is ridden with unpleasant, almost impenetrable, conflict.

Though most students of psychology and education are doubtless familiar with Freud's tri-partite division of personality, i.e., the Id, Ego, and Superego, it may be helpful to explicate these theoretical constructs to show how they shed light on his theory of moral development.

Freud characterizes the *Id* as representative of animal-like instinctual impulses (largely of an unconscious sexual nature), the very core of human being and the repository for primary thought process. In essence, the Id signifies what we primordially desire to do if there were in fact no restrictions on our desires. These desires are most clearly demonstrable in dreams, fantasies, and similar unconscious thought phenomena. Freud further hypothesizes that the Id plays a predominant role in infancy and early childhood development, a period he considers most crucial in the overall development of the individual.

To counter-balance the Id, Freud introduces the term *Ego* to signify that self-regulating product of secondary (more conscious and rational) thought process which serves to bring the Id under some tenuous executory control. However, ego functions are refined only slowly and gradually, as the child grows and matures.

Most important for moral development in Freud's psychology is the role of the *Superego*, i.e., the inhibiting, restraining, prohibiting standards imposed on the child by outside social forces, initially and primarily by one's parents and later by teachers and other adult authority figures. From such parental and other external social sources, the child, if s/he is to be "normal" and "adjusted," develops an *ego-ideal* and *conscience*. Indeed, for Freud, guilt operating via the conscience is a form of "social glue" which cements, as it were, the cultural bonds of any society. Without guilt and conscience, life would degenerate into a "tooth-and-nail" existence and attendant societal chaos. Of course, according to Freud's psychic balancing scheme, excessive guilt disables individual action and may well lead to "neurotic," even "psychotic," behavior.

On the whole, however, Freud points to an optimal realization of self-control through an almost stoical exertion of rationality. He invokes such individual self-control because he contends that a substantial measure of repression is necessary to balance man's psychic apparatus, especially id impulses, with the demands of culture. Freud thus employs the concept of "repression" to regulate the seemingly irreconcilable conflict between individual autonomy and cultural restraint.

The term *repression* is used by Freud to express that most general, largely unconscious, defense mechanism which enables us to keep out of consciousness those thoughts, wishes, and desires too dangerous to one's conscious mental processes. A form of repression, *sublimation* refers to that defense mechanism which transforms id-like excitations into more socially acceptable patterns of behavior. Indeed, for Freud, sublimation serves to build culture in the form of art, religion, literature, etc. Accordingly, he calls upon man to sublimate what he assumes to be primary aggressive sex instincts with what is deemed necessary to constitute civilization:

> Civilization thus obtains mastery over the dangerous love of aggression in individuals by enfeebling and disarming it, and setting up an institution [superego] within their minds to keep watch over it, like a garrison in a conquered city.[1]

The demands of civilized life require man to struggle *with* repression, i.e., to practice a kind of frustrating, "heroic" individualism. To do otherwise would imperil cultural cohesion, which would, in turn, endanger individual man. This scenario summarizes Freud's version of "enlightened self-interest."

Even more significantly, this synopsis of Freud's psychology reveals how tenuous all morality is in Freud's eyes: it is a function of sublimations of the libido, i.e., those erotic, instinctual motive forces which presumably lay at the root of all human thinking and all human values. Freud traces such "higher" impulses largely to the superego in this very telling passage:

> It is easy to show that the ego ideal [of the superego] answers to everything that is expected of the higher nature of man. As a substitute for a

---

[1]Freud, Sigmund: *Civilization and Its Discontents*, J. Strachey (Tr.). New York, Norton, 1961, p. 105.

longing for the father, it contains the germ from which all religions [and moral systems] have evolved. The self-judgment which declares that the ego falls short of its ideal produces the religious sense of humility to which the believer appeals in his longing. As a child grows up, the role of father is carried on by teachers and others in authority; their injunctions and prohibitions remain powerful in the ego ideal and continue, in the form of conscience, to exercise the moral censorship. The tension between the demands of conscience and the actual performances of the ego is experienced as a sense of guilt. Social feelings rest on identification with other people, on the basis of having the same ego-ideal.[2]

According to Seymour Fox, who has written a useful treatise on Freud's personality theory for education,[3] Freud's notions on moral development can be schematized in terms of how one's ego ideal organizes and interprets the so-called "higher" thought processes:

(1) religion = longing for father
(2) censorship and morality = sense of worthlessness
(3) submission to authority
(4) social feeling = identification with those with similar ego ideal

Given Freud's highly creative, but equally speculative, claims — most of which deal in *intrapsychic* phenomena seemingly immune to any inter-subjective public testing — one cannot help but inquire: From what sources does Freud's theory of morality originate in the first place? The response to that sobering question will hardly mollify more empirically-minded investigators. Resuscitating ancient mythology and Greek dramaturgy, Freud casts the foundation stones of morality in the parable of the "primal horde" and the tragedy of Oedipus and Electra. In the primal-horde parable, the sons of a clan commit patricide in order to replace the feared,

---

[2]Freud, Sigmund: The ego and the id. In J. Strachey (Ed.): *The Standard Edition of the Complete Psychological Works of Sigmund Freud*. London, Hogarth, vol. XIX, 1953-1966, p. 37. Presaging his pupil Jung's interest in unconscious "archetypes," Freud also relies on the power and urgency of the phylogenetic past: "The . . . tradition of the race and of the people, lives on in the ideologies of the super-ego, and yields only slowly to the influences of the present and to new changes . . ." Freud, Sigmund: New introductory lectures on psychoanalysis. *Ibid.*, vol. XXII, p. 67. This interest in the conservative phylogenetic past would also be carried on by G. Stanley Hall in America.

[3]Fox, Seymour: *Freud and Education*. Springfield, Thomas, 1975, p. 224.

dominating father figure. In terms of Oedipus and Electra, Freud hypothesizes that young boys fear castration and thus internalize and identify with father. In a certain sense, then, it is fear of castration which permits growth in morality in the male child's youthful development.

Feminist readers have long been suspicious of Freud's treatment of the Electra complex since it appears to place women in a much more precarious, problematic role. On Freud's terms, it becomes a psychological impossibility for girls to achieve a strong sense of morality because of what he assumes to be weaker superego development in females.[4] Unlike boys, who presumably fear castration and thus undergo value-internalization and value-identification through "castration anxiety," girls are already, as it were, "castrated" and cannot experience the same fears and threat of loss. As a consequence of this predicament, Freud postulates that young girls develop "penis envy," a very controversial notion which is still under severe attack by some less orthodox analysts, both feminist and non-feminist.[5]

For instance, Elizabeth Janeway's critical commentary on Freud's views echoes some of the reservations of later observers:

> Freud himself occasionally warned [in his essay on "Femininity"] . . . against the "superimposition" of unjustified significance on the facts of physical differences between the sexes. But these differences are just what he cites to account for the social roles of men and women, even though anyone reading him today can follow his arguments perfectly well (indeed better) by taking these differences as *symbolic* of assigned gender roles . . . of the socialization process of learning and accepting norms of behavior and expression.[6]

Adding further fuel to feminist criticism is the particular spotlight in which women are obliged to play their role in Freud's unfolding moral drama. Woman is viewed as the temptress and scorner of civilization, the Eve-like character who squanders men's attempts to

---

[4]Freud, Sigmund: New introductory lectures on psychoanalysis. In *Standard Edition*, vol. XXII, p. 166.

[5]See the next section on Adler and Chapter 5 of this text, especially Carol Gilligan's counter-paradigm to the Freudian-Kohlbergian tradition in psychological theory.

[6]Janeway, Elizabeth: *Cross Sections: From a Decade of Change.* New York, Morrow, 1982, pp. 78-79. See also Freud: *Three Essays on the Theory of Sexuality* (1905), J. Strachey (Tr.). New York, Basic, 1962.

sublimate their psychic energy, which is not limitless, into "higher" cultural tasks:

> The next discord is caused by women, who soon become antithetical to cultural trends, and spread around them their conservative influence — the women who at the beginning laid the foundation of culture by the appeal of their love. Women represent the interests of the family and the sexual life; the work of civilization has become more and more men's business; it confronts them with even harder tasks, compels them to sublimations of instinct which women are not easily able to achieve. Since man has not an unlimited amount of mental energy at his disposal, he must accomplish his tasks by distributing his libido to the best advantage. What he employs for cultural purposes he withdraws to a great extent from women and his sexual life.[7]

This lengthy quotation reveals several troublesome features in Freudian thought:

(1) its superimposition of an outmoded Newtonian (energy) model of physics onto psychic life;

(2) a bifurcation of the instincts and rationality in another classic Western formulation of "lower" and "higher" thought functions, assuming those functions can be so easily divided;

(3) a resultant positing of frustration for *both* men and women, the locus of that frustration resting on the roles assigned to the players; and

(4) Freud's almost imperceptible admission that those roles may be more or less changeable, after all (i.e., his "Freudian slip" to the effect that "civilization *has become* more and more men's business").[8]

Freud's own student, Alfred Adler, would eventually come to the conclusion that Freud was unable to view the *social* context surrounding women's dilemma. Adler noted that dominant cultural groups and institutions, male or otherwise, are slow to remove blinders which bestow certain prerogatives of definitional power. He would also observe, with Georg Simmel, that other inhabitants of culture, seeking after solutions for social cohesion and personal solace, would mirror and accept such "authoritative" interpretations as if they were "universal" and "objective" guides to heart and mind for

---

[7]Freud: *Civilization and Its Discontents*, p. 73.

[8]For an incisive account of Freud's apparent inability to concede the full socio-historic underpinnings and implications of his own thought, see Marcuse, Herbert: *Eros and Civilization: A Philosophical Inquiry into Freud*. New York, Vintage, 1962.

generations to come:

> The requirements of art, patriotism, morality in general and social
> ideals in particular, correctness in practical judgment and objectivity in
> theoretical knowledge, the energy and the profundity of life — all these
> are categories which belong as it were in their form and their claims to
> humanity in general, but in their actual historical configuration they are
> masculine throughout. Supposing that we describe these things, viewed
> as absolute ideas, by the single word "objective," we then find that in the
> history of our race the equation objective = masculine is a valid one.[9]

Thus, it became Adler's task to confront Freud's psycho-
biological model of morality. Subsequent theorists would come to regard Adler's critique as part of a "minority," or dissenting, view in
academic psychology. Lately, this minority camp of psychologists
and educators has begun to question what they term the fundamental "theoretical egocentrism" of Freudian and certain post-Freudian
paradigms, including that of Kohlberg. For example, Robert Hogan
argues that the dominant thrust of contemporary psychological
theory has tended to wed Western thought to an "individualistic"
perspective, thereby submerging such issues as "cooperation" and
"social equality."[10] Such critics contend that these dominant models
focus primarily on *internal*, *individual*, and *differential* measures of man
and morality in their reliance on such constructs as "genetic deficiencies," "weak superegos," and "pre/post/conventional personalities"
(Kohlberg).[11] As a result of such theoretical constructions, a certain
set of preconceptions about the nature of human beings, their morality, and the possibilites (or impossibilities) of socio-educational
change begins to emerge. These formulations tend to "blame the victim," rather than the larger social order, for any obstacle or difficulty
that the individual cannot overcome.

---

[9]Simmel, Georg: *Philosophische Kultur*, as quoted in Horney, Karen: The flight from wom-
anhood: The masculinity-complex in women as viewed by men and by women. In
Kelman, H. (Ed.): *Feminine Psychology*. New York, Norton, 1967, pp. 55-56.

[10]Hogan, Robert: Theoretical egocentrism and the problem of compliance. *American Psychologist*, 30:533-540, 1975.

[11]William Ryan explores the enormous ramifications in public policy on social and moral
issues generated by internal, intrapsychic paradigms in his *Blaming the Victim*. New York,
Pantheon, 1976; and *Equality*. New York, Pantheon, 1981.

In the next section, we will look at Adler's often overlooked views on morality in an effort to clarify why and how he attempted to dislodge his master's theory and therapy. (Ironically, the relative neglect of Adler in academic psychology is also evident in Carol Gilligan's contemporary feminist paradigm of moral development. Gilligan never mentions Adler in her pioneering research although his theory, as will be shown, serves to foreshadow major themes in Gilligan's work.)

An appropriate place to conclude our study of Freud and to begin our elaboration of Adler is this candid confession of Freud—one which introduces us to Adler's serious misgivings about psychoanalytic theory and practice, particularly its characterization of "enlightened self-interest":

> In the years before the war, . . . I [Freud] made it a rule never to take for treatment anyone who was not *sui juis*, independent of others in all the essential relations of life.[12]

ADLER: SOCIAL INTEREST

Freud's original disciple, Adler, broke away from his teacher to form his own school ("Individual Psychology") on the ground that Freud's theory of sexuality was too reductionistic and that psychoanalytic dependence on "aggressive drives" posited an overly deterministic, largely intrapsychic and biological, view of human nature. In essence, Adler proposed to avoid any such reductionism and determinism by formulating a dialectical account of social dynamics and social relationships. Though Adler also emphasizes the importance of the early years of development, he is much more concerned with *social* influences which impinge upon thought, action, and behavior. Indeed, Adler's overarching theory of "social interest" places the whole range of viewing human behavior and

---

[12]Freud: *Introductory Lectures on Psycho-Analysis*. New York, Norton, 1929, pp. 385-386. Before World War I, sexual instincts were crucial in Freud's theory; thereafter, aggression and death instinct (Thanatos) seemed to become as critical. In either case, man was still viewed from an *internal* psychic lens, i.e., his motivations and determinant behavior appeared to lurk from *within* the individual.

morality in an entirely different perspective. Since Adler's major contributions have been somewhat submerged in the history of psychology and because his views of morality are unsystematic, it will be necessary to articulate those Adlerian concepts which seem particularly crucial to any exposition and assessment of his theory for moral development.

Adler claims that all humans enter the world in a position of "inferiority," i.e., we are all relatively helpless and dependent in infancy. From this original station in life, we gradually "strive toward overcoming" a feeling of powerlessness.[13] The conceptual vehicle by which Adler explains the progression from inferiority to "strivings for superiority" as one grows and matures has long been a prickly source of confusion, contention, and misconstruction among students in psychology. Adler borrowed Nietzsche's term "will to power" to describe how humans could "perfect" their existence, not to depict any yearnings for power and authority over other persons. In fact, on Adler's terms, any such egocentric striving would be viewed as "neurotic" and counter-productive to his own value system, which stressed "cooperation" as a prime motivating force, perhaps the most necessary human invention, in man's evolution. In some of his writings, Adler makes this point in clearer fashion:

> [The task of life is] to show the way in the reduction of the striving for personal power and in the education toward the community . . . and the development of social interest.[14]

In Adler's theory, then, "inferiority" and "power," properly defined, are integral to a fuller explanation of his most important principle, "social interest," which he characterizes as "compensation for all the natural weaknesses of individual human beings."[15] Social interest encompasses communal feeling, interpersonality, and empathy for others. According to Adler, the history of mankind is a movement toward more socially "superior," cooperative, and demo-

---

[13]Adler, Alfred: *Co-operation Between the Sexes: Writings on Women and Men, Love and Marriage, and Sexuality*, Ansbacher, Heinz L. and Rowena R. (Eds.). New York, Norton, 1978, pp. 49, 147-148, 168-169.

[14]Adler: *The Nervous Character: Fundamentals of a Comparative Individual Psychology and Psychotherapy*, 4th ed. Munich, Bergmann, 1928, pp. iv-vi.

[15]Adler: *Problems of Neurosis*. London, Kegan Paul, 1929, p. 31.

cratic directions necessitating equality in all aspects of life.[16] Indeed, he and his major disciple, Rudolf Dreikurs, use the standard of "social interest" to judge the extent to which culture and individual personality have "matured":

> The degree of a person's social interest determines his ability and willingness to function socially; the lack of social interest is at the root of deficiencies, failures, and pathology. Thus, Adler found that social interest was a gauge for defining normalcy, both for the individual and for the group.[17]

Adlerians conceive of social interest as both inborn and capable of nurture and development as the child grows and matures. Accordingly, children should be given social tasks and responsibilities to perform, depending on their level of maturity. Household chores, family helping, and school duties, as examples, breed those patterns of behavior which eventually instill habits of both interdependence and independence in children. Paralleling Freud's concern for "reality testing" through ego strengthening, Adlerians admonish against "pampering," a practice they regard as injurious as child abuse or neglect.[18] For instance, an isolate, self-centered "princely" child bears little mark of that indelible imprint of social interest which Adlerians insist is required for the continuous growth of mankind as a whole and for that person as a self-sustaining individual:

> The very concept of "human being" includes our entire understanding of social feeling . . . . [We have] always lived in groups, unless separated from one another artificially or through insanity . . . . In the deepest sense, the feeling for the logic of human living together is social feeling . . .[19]

With specific reference to early development, Dreikurs notes that "the child, at any age level, is a typical human being who wants his place in the group and rebels against being subdued."[20] Taking up Adler's work, Dreikurs extends the notion of "social interest" to include "social equality" and democratic alignments among all per-

---

[16]Adler: *Social Interest: Challenge to Mankind* (1938). New York, Capricorn, 1964.
[17]Dreikurs, Rudolf: *Social Equality: The Challenge of Today.* Chicago, Regnery, 1971, p. viii.
[18]Dreikurs and Soltz, Vicki: *Children: The Challenge.* New York, Hawthorn, 1964. This interest in "reality testing" is also reflected in the work of Freud's other pupil, C.G. Jung.
[19]Adler: *Co-operation Between the Sexes*, p. 107.
[20]Dreikurs: *Social Equality*, p. 80.

sons, regardless of their station in life. Indeed, he describes egalitarian relationships as the "only stable basis for [any] social relationships."[21]

However, the apparent thrust of Adlerian arguments for democratic cooperation as an approximate ideal of human behavior is not meant to discount adult guidance of the child. Though Adlerians stress the importance of generating egalitarian conditions, they grant the necessity of significant adult presence in assuring the evolution of a discernible, not chaotic, social order. For that matter, they insist that "learning respect for order" is essential for establishing stability and rationality in the child's surroundings.[22] (In this sense, Adlerians seem not too far removed from Durkheim's traditional adult role model of moral development. The Adlerian reliance on adult authority also underlines a critical difference in its theory and practice as opposed to that of Piaget, who argues that peer interaction can substitute effectively for such adult supervision. Research for and against Piaget's position is discussed subsequently.) Evidently, Adlerians, like many parents, have noticed that even young children have been known to "read" and manipulate their elders. Consequently, a primary task of Adlerian family therapy becomes that of assisting parents and teachers in locating and rechanneling children's "faulty" motivations (and "mistaken behavior") in more "socially useful" directions.

Dreikurs attempts to balance the extremes of "authoritarian" and "permissive" child rearing through the use of the learning device, "natural and logical consequences":

> What would be the natural consequences of forgetting one's lunch? One would go hungry . . . This is the natural consequence of her forgetfulness.[23]
>
> Consequences, which must be natural and logical to the disturbances of order, are self-evident . . . it is order and reality . . . not the arbitrary power of adults, which brings about the unpleasant consequences.[24]

Some critics have characterized this Adlerian teaching tool as "an

---

[21]*Ibid.*, p. 115.

[22]Dreikurs and Soltz: *Children: The Challenge*, pp. 96-102.

[23]*Ibid.*, p. 76.

[24]Dreikurs: The cultural impliations of reward and punishment. *International Journal of Social Psychiatry*, 4:177, 1948

interesting deployment of 'intentions' and 'consequences' " but one which tends, in reality, to subordinate the autonomy of the learner to parental and environmental influence, i.e., a measure which parallels behavioral forms of child rearing.[25]

Yet the Adlerian interest in addressing subordinate/superordinate relationships does generate promise for growth in democratic and social morality, particularly in the case of the sexes. For Adler, unequal sexual relationships constituted a bone of contention, an unwritten "power struggle," as it were, for both sexes. Accordingly, he advocated the "equal worth of the sexes":

> Women have to suffer because in our culture it is much easier for a man
> to play the leading role. But the man also suffers because by this ficti-
> tious [spurious] superiority he loses touch with the underlying values.[26]

Adler coined the term *masculine protest* to express the feeling which either sex experiences in contexts involving inferior/superior social interactions and distinctions. Another widely misunderstood Adlerian concept, *masculine protest* implied a present, but changeable, condition of "feminine" traits, principally a feeling of inferiority as a result of given, not necessary, social conditions of male domination. Adler envisioned an evolving antithesis to this condition in the form of "strivings for superiority" which would be refined and perfected to the point of overcoming subordinate or oppressive circumstances.[27]

Thus Adler viewed "masculine protest" as a culturally-biased criterion favorable to males, and not on the basis of physiolgocial sex differentiation. His standard implied that sexual distinctions were largely the result of unnecessary *social* determinations, not biological necessities. In this connection, it is interesting to speculate upon that intriguing distinction made by one of Freud's major recent revisionists, Herbert Marcuse. The latter uses the concepts "basic" versus "surplus" repression to clarify those kinds of repressive measures

---

[25]DeVitis, Joseph L.: Cooperation and social equality in chidhood: Adlerian and Piagetian lessons. *Journal of Research and Development in Education*, 17:23, 1984.

[26]Adler: *The Education of Children*. New York, Greenberg, 1930, p. 222.

[27]Ansbacher: In Adler, *Co-operation Between the Sexes*, pp. 155-156, 162-164. Freud castigated Adler's notion of "masculine protest," couching it as a veiled reflection and consequent deflection of "universal castration anxiety" and common aggressive propensities. See Freud: Analysis terminable and interminable. In Strachey, James (Ed.): *The Collected Papers of Sigmund Freud*. New York, Basic, 1950, vol. V, p. 357n.

which are necessary and unnecessary. "Basic" repression refers to that modification of the "instincts necessary for the perpetuation of the human race in civilization," e.g., provision of food and shelter and combatting of disease. "Surplus" repression refers to those additive "restrictions necessitated by social domination," i.e., layered forms of constraint over and above that which is essential to the maintenance of civilized life. According to Marcuse, surplus-repression has been caused by socio-historic conditions, which are amenable to social change.[28] The point to be made in the Freud/Adler dispute is that Adler seems to have recognized Marcuse's distinctions in ways which Freud did not:

> In our society, an exaggerated importance is attached to masculinity, and the inferiority of the female sex is assumed as a generally established principle. Even if sexual equality is admitted theoretically, [social] actions . . . usually speak the contrary . . . . From the earliest days the child is led to believe that the male is the more valuable sex.[29]

Consequently, Adler attempted to reduce the strife and competition attending these unequal and oppressive social conditions. Unlike Freud, who was very dubious of social change, Adler participated in social reform. For example, he organized child guidance clinics and experimental schools throughout Austria.[30]

This curious development allows us to find clues to such conclusions in the manner in which Freud and Adler conceived of (1) their own therapeutic practice and (2) their analysis of the role and scope of the family and other social institutions. Whereas Freudian therapy emphasizes the primacy of the analyst as a distant, but authoritative, figure, Adlerians stress the import of fostering social interest via the client's own "expert" private logic and intentions. And whereas self-insight is a sufficient end in psychoanalytic psychiatry, it is usually insufficient, sometimes unnecessary, in Individual Psychology.

---

[28]Marcuse: *Eros and Civilization*, pp. 32-34.

[29]Way, Lewis: *Adler's Place in Psychology: An Exposition of Individual Psychology*. New York, Collier, 1962, p. 34.

[30]Dreikurs: Early experiments in social psychiatry. *International Journal of Social Psychiatry*, 7:141-147, 1961; Papanek, Ernst: *The Austrian School Reform*. New York, Fell, 1962; and DeVitis, Joseph L.: Freud, Adler, and women: powers of the "weak" and "strong," *Educational Theory*, in press.

The goal of Adlerian counseling is to move the client into the *social* arena since most seemingly psychological problems are viewed, by Adlerians, as primarily *social* problems. Freud's predominantly internal, intrapsychic perspective fails to grasp this point fully. For Adlerians, change in behavior is an essential clue to any growth in self-insight, i.e., basing one's judgment solely on "thoughts, desires, and emotions [fails] to give sufficient . . . consideration [to] our actions—to what we *do*.[31] Indeed, some therapists have argued that excessive self-analysis could conceivably ignite a flight into various forms of pathology (e.g., narcissism and paranoia).[32]

Other critics have leveled a more basic attack on the manner in which psychoanalysts conceptualize all human relations, particularly family structures. These observers make the case that psychoanalysis tends to reduce human relations to the level and pattern of the psyche within the substructure of the nuclear family. In their view, Freud tended to collapse all social action so as to picture it as a recapitulation of emotional sets within the mental frame of the family. As such, according to this critique, Freud erroneously universalizes certain internalized family matrices, thus disabling him from weighing—or even seeing—the impact of overarching, perhaps more dominant, external social structures of particular times and places (in his case, patriarchal Victorian society):

> The hero [Freudian man] is able to attain to "individual psychology" only because he internalizes his father at a deep enough level; he creates an "ego-ideal" in himself. Hence the mechanism for reproducing individuals—those who are free, who can think, who can restrain their emotions, who can be distinctive—is the key to history . . . [and] the mechanism for this degree of individualization is the patriarchal nuclear family.[33]

Cultural and literary critics have depicted Freud's characterization of morality as "enlightened self-interest" in more comical, but deadly serious and tragic, overtones:

> The aim of Freudian psychiatry is . . . the reconciliation of instinct and

---

[31]Dreikurs: On knowing oneself. *International Journal of Individual Psychology*, 3:13-23, 1937.
[32]Laing, R.D.: *The Divided Self*. New York, Pantheon, 1969.
[33]Poster, Mark: *Critical Theory of the Family*. New York, Seabury, 1980, pp. 34-35. Cf. Freud: *Group Psychology and the Analysis of the Ego*, J. Strachey (Tr.). New York, Norton, 1965.

intelligence. The intellect is set to helping the instincts develop, toler-
antly, like a prudent teacher. Conscience, however, directs us to repress
the instincts. The conscience-stricken thus do not appear by Freudian
standards to be very intelligent. By viewing conscience as in opposition
to intelligence, Freud exhibits a prejudice against virtue fairly common
among secular intellectuals—the idea that the merely good person is not
likely to be either very clever or very strong.[34]
[In] the suppression of an overactive conscience by the rest of the mind
. . . the leader most prompt to appear . . . [is] Enlightened Self-
Interest . . . It is essentially the black and white Jolly Roger, with these
words written beneath the skull and crossbar, "The hell with you, Jack,
I've got mine!" [Thus] . . . a normal person, functioning well on the upper levels of a prosperous, industrialized society, can hardly hear his
conscience at all.[35]

Given this doleful state of affairs, Vonnegut, the novelist, can locate only a rare few individuals, usually branded as "fools" by the
larger society, "who reach biological maturity still loving and wanting to help their fellow men."[36]

The essential point of this cultural and literary excursion has
been to show the strain of morality which is apparently missing in
Freudian theory and therapy and to exemplify how Adler presages
present moral paradigms which consider the primacy of "sympathy,
compassion, and human concern."[37] It is in this light that Adler can
be seen rightly as a forerunner to some of the kernel ideas in Gilligan's current feminist model of moral development—one which sup-
ports a moral language of care, responsibility, and not wanting to
hurt others.[38] Indeed, a reacquaintance with Adler might actually
serve to extend Gilligan's thesis in that the latter tends to speak solely
of *private* social relationships (e.g., family members, friends, and colleagues) rather than a larger social community.[39]

[34]Rieff, Philip: *Freud: The Mind of the Moralist.* Garden City, Doubleday, 1959, pp. 305-306.
[35]Vonnegut, Kurt, Jr.: *God Bless You, Mr. Rosewater: Or Pearls Before Swine.* New York, Dell,
1965, pp. 42-43.
[36]*Ibid.*
[37]Blum, Lawrence A.: *Friendship, Altruism and Morality.* London, Routledge and Kegan
Paul, 1980.
[38]Gilligan, Carol: *In A Different Voice: Psychological Theory and Women's Development.* Cambridge:
Harvard U.P., 1982.
[39]Sichel, Betty A.: Moral development and education: men's language of rights and wom-
en's language of responsibility. *Contemporary Education Review*, 2:33-42, 1983.

Thus Adler's theory highlights other possible perspectives, e.g., those of *collective* and *external* reference, which certain critics claim have been submerged in the history of psychology.[40] In David Bakan's more recent terminology, Adler points to possibilites for *communal* as well as merely "agentic" (self/power) development.[41]

All this is not meant to convey the impression that Adler was theorizing without moral or social blinders. Throughout much of his writing, Adler appears to be unaware that he is commiting the naturalistic fallacy in argumentation by mixing claims for "is" and "ought." In many ways, his theory is couched in prescriptive terms which he would like to maintain are purely descriptive:

> Individual Psychology . . . regards as "right" that which is useful for the community . . . . Every departure from the social standard is an offense against right and brings with it a conflict with the objective laws and objective necessities of reality . . . . [It] violates an immanent social ideal which everyone of us, consciously or unconsciously, carries in himself.[42]

In addition, Adler's social analysis is lacking in rigor, depth, and precision. That is to say, his account of interpersonal social relationships does not elaborate fully the larger, more amorphous, power structures and sociopolitical constraints which more recent critics have observed.[43] Nor does he entirely fathom the deep-seated imponderables which might make for well-nigh irreconcilable conflict, as Freud himself recognized so well. As an example, Adler fails to distinguish adequately the boundaries between social "cooperation" and social "constraint" or "conformity."[44]

---

[40]In his *Equality*, Ryan elucidates these individual/internal versus collective/external distinctions in clear, common-sense fashion. Freud took collective action to be largely "regressive" and antithetical to intelligent self-restraint. See Poster: *Critical Theory of the Family*, pp. 37-38.

[41]Bakan, David: *The Duality of Human Existence*. Chicago, Rand McNally, 1966. See also Sampson, Edward E.: Psychology and the American ideal. *Journal of Personality and Social Psychology*, 35:767-782, 1977.

[42]Adler: *The Education of Children*, p. 21.

[43]Jacoby, Russell: *Social Amnesia: A Critique of Contemporary Psychology from Adler to Laing*. Boston, Beacon, 1976.

[44]DeVitis: Cooperation and social equality in childhood: Adlerian and Piagetian lessons, p. 24.

At base, both Freud and Adler are relying upon theoretical constructs — be they "aggressive instincts" (Freud) or "cooperation" (Adler) — which have not been conclusively warranted in either clinical or experimental studies. Perforce it is extremely difficult to prove that propensities of any sort are "built into" human nature — a monumental point of controversy at least since John Locke introduced his notion of "tabula rasa" (blank slate) in the 17th century and radically challenged classical conceptions of man's "goodness" or "evil." (Of course, future theorists and practitioners — from Carl Rogers to sociobiologists — would continue to make such assumptions about the nature of man, however far apart their differentiations and distinctions on such matters as "altruism" and "aggression" might take them.)[45]

JUNG: FROM FANTASY TO REALITY

Carl Jung, another of Freud's original disciples and apostates, does not formulate a systematic account of the contours and nuances of moral development. Indeed, moral growth is assumed by Jung to be a lifelong process which results in "self-actualization" for relatively few individuals only by the time they reach middle age or beyond. Nevertheless, Jung's insights into child maturation will be focused on in this section for the richness of sources he brings to bear on wide ranging issues and because of the imaginative, if not always convincing, way in which he views the child's inner struggle to come to grips with collectivity and individuality. Once again, we are dealing with a psychological theorist who is bent on synthesizing the elements of stability and autonomy.

Jung's intense interest in archaeology, anthropology, and religion led him to study primitive artifacts from various cultures which seemed to have traits in common, e.g., the adoration of the Virgin, or Mother, figure as well as universal curiosities attached to the Circle (Mandala). From such exploration, Jung concluded that human forces derive primordially from a collective base and that all men

[45]See, for example, Rogers, Carl R.: *On Becoming a Person*. Boston, Houghton Mifflin, 1961; and Wilson, Edward O.: *On Human Nature*. New York, Bantam, 1979.

share certain core components from that human condition. At root, this primitive collective sharing rests in the unconscious. The task of moral development is to differentiate those components of the unconscious which will make for a balanced psychic life, to eventually enable the conscious personality to become self-regulating and unified in all its parts.[46] In psychodynamic terms, Jung's neo-analytic mission is that of permitting the relatively impersonal collective unconscious to be refined to the point that it is appropriated by one's personal ego.

For the child, this development follows along the lines of a very gradual shifting from fantasy to reality; and this unfolding is ascertained by one's ability to distinguish those two realms:

> Development starts from a condition of complete participation in, and undifferentiation from, the inner [fantasy] and outer [real] world in which it lives; it then proceeds by way of the development of its ego, and the separation of its personality from its anonymous identity with all existing facts. That is why the word "I" only enters the consciousness of the child comparatively late, towards the end of the third year of life; a sign that it is only then that the first appreciable and conscious traces of an ego-personality as opposed to the collective psyche appears.[47]

The most primitive traces of the developing psyche, for Jung, are located in what he terms the "archetypes," symbolic representations of those instinctual clusters of ideas which have been formed unconsciously over the centuries. They are part of one's personal as well as collective unconscious and allow the child to draw, as it were, "self-portraits" of his/her instincts so that s/he can imagine and perfect his idea of certain mental constructs, e.g., "mother," "father," and the like.[48] Jolan Jacobi, still perhaps the most lucid interpreter of Jung's

----

[46]Notice should be taken of Jung's similarities with Freud and Durkheim. With Freud, Jung emphasizes the primacy of the unconscious, though his use of anthropological evidence leads him to develop a separate category for the *collective* unconscious — to some critics, an illustration of highly mystical constructs which have been a principal source of reaction against Jung. With Durkehim (though he never mentions him), Jung is attempting to integrate the competing interests of the collective and the individual into an ongoing "self-regulating" system.

[47]Adler, Gerhard: *Studies in Analytical Psychology.* New York: Putnam, 1967, p. 127.

[48]Classical scholars will note Jung's borrowing of this conception from St. Augustine's notion of "reminiscence," an idea later re-translated by Plato to mean "primordial image," or the "essence" of reality. Jung's treatment of archetypes also places him in the psychological tradition which insists that ontogeny (the single individual organism) recapitulates phylogeny (the group, species, or race) — a very debatable theory made more explicit in G. Stanley Hall's studies of adolescence.

psychology, gives this illustration of the role and scope of archetypes:

> For example, the archetype "Mother" is . . . pre-existent and superordinate to every form of manifestation of the "motherly." It is a constant core of meaning, which can take on all the aspects and symbols of the "motherly." The primordial image of the mother and the characteristics of the "Great Mother" with all her paradoxical traits are the same in the soul of present-day man as in mythological times . . . . Realizing or becoming conscious means . . . forming a world by drawing distinctions [among such traits and characteristics].[49]

Thus, according to Jung, the maturation process becomes one of restructuring and integrating fantasy life to make it complementary with "real" life through an ongoing broadening of consciousness. The child must inevitably separate himself from the "land of childhood" (fantasy) by employing reason, melding it to his earlier "historical soul" (archetypes) and largely instinctual existence. At the same time, throughout life, the compensating features of instinct and reason, fantasy and reality, must be assimilated constantly if man is to live a whole, unified life. That is to say, the instinctual resources of childhood ideally provide a perennial flow of life force; without them, mature man takes on a "dried up," sterile, overly rationalized visage.[50] After all, it is fantasy which breeds creativity and sensitive reflection.

This picture of the slowly unfolding personality allows us to see how Jung visualizes the manner in which divergent kinds of thinking, apparently so crucial in moral reasoning, develop. Even by way of the primitive archetypes, the child is beginning to experience, in some respects, how others before him have acted and judged life. In this fashion, s/he will gradually learn to discern similarities and differences in humanity, i.e., how and why men have lived collectively and individually. Through such learning, later critical distinctions can be made — distinctions which may eventuate in a psychic life of freedom from the crowd and an integrated view of how cooperative

[49]Jacobi, Jolan: *The Psychology of Jung*, K.W. Bash (Tr.). New Haven: Yale U.P., 1943, pp. 44-45.

[50]In this regard, Jung is critical of the Western penchant to "over-differentiate" consciousness. He was more hopeful that Oriental culture would offer a more compensating balance between the conscious and the unconscious, as in the practice of meditation. See Jung: *The Integration of the Personality*, S.M. Dell (Tr.). London: Kegan Paul, 1940, p. 106.

social life can also be morally beneficial.

To recap Jung's theory, let us return to the specifics of his developmental model. Though the first few years of life are as significant to Jung as they are to his master Freud, Jung likewise insists that there is little conscious development during those years (thus his rationale for minimizing the use of psychotherapy with young children). The child remains largely unconscious to himself from ages 1-3; during which time s/he exhibits many manifestations of an animal creature.[51] "Only when the child begins to say "I" [at approximately 3-5 years of age] is there any perceptible continuity of consciousness."[52] In effect, s/he is developing consciousness of his/her ego. It is generally at puberty that youth grow in the direction of independence.

During childhood the role of the school can be vital in refining and taming instincts, differentiating youth from their more "primitive" impulses, i.e., making them more compatible with civilized existence. In this regard, Jung seems to be implicitly echoing much of Durkheim's argument for the necessity of socialization. Like Durkheim, he emphasizes that the teacher influences mainly as a role model by the force of his/her personality. The teacher also serves to wean the child from overdependence on his/her parents and the immediate environment.

What kind of educational development would Jung recommend? His response is consistent with his general theory of the "integrated personality." Jung believes firmly in the importance of a broad liberal education, one in which the humanities are the central activity and content of the curriculum. He warns roundly against overspecialization and a disregard for the mistakes of the past. In short, Jung is committed to a developmental education in which past roots can be gradually and naturally embedded in the child's present and future life, ideally allowing him/her a total integration of the uncon-

---

[51]Once again, Jung intimates, along with G.S. Hall, that individuals evolve through the same stages, from "primitive" to "progressive" forms, as their species. Jung's "animal" characterization is also remindful of Piaget's description of the predominantly "egocentric" traits of early childhood.

[52]Jung: The development of personality: papers on child psychology, education, and related subjects. In R.F.C. Hull (Tr.): *Collected Papers of C.G. Jung*. New York, Pantheon, 1954, vol. 17, p. 52.

scious and conscious, the world of fantasy melding into the experience of reality.[53]

Specifically, Jung divides the developmental span of education into three parts: (1) education through example; (2) collective education; and (3) individual education. These roughly parallel the progression from unconscious education to more individuated, consciously differentiated, education as the person matures and balances his/her own personality.

By "education through example," Jung concerns himself with those early stages of child development when the young person is "more or less identical with its environment, and especially with its parents," that period in which s/he is still struggling to mold his/her primitive, largely unconscious, psyche. Though this mode of development ultimately gives way to collective and individual education, Jung is insistent on the primacy of "contagion through experience" in building psychic identity throughout his pedagogic agenda.[54]

Jung's translation of "collective" education is not to be confused with mass schooling. Instead it refers to adherence to certain general rules, principles, and methodologies in order to establish a modicum of uniformity in the culture. However, Jung's version of socialization does not call for a "lock-step" form of uniformity which would crush unique individuality. As such, Jung is concerned that personhood be protected in the security of individual judgments—many of which may not have recourse to rules and regulations. In this, he seems to be searching, albeit unsystematically and willy-nilly, for those same kinds of safeguards on autonomy which interested and counfounded Durkheim. Unfortunately, Jung likewise makes no concrete recommendations for such securities on self-determination.[55]

As the pupil grows and matures, "individual" education takes on

---

[53]*Ibid.*, pp. 144-145. Of course, some critics have challenged Jung's allegiance to "past roots" on the ground that such a notion may have influenced his flirtation with Nazism. This issue may be part and parcel of the same socialization question which was seen to plague Durkheim earlier.

[54]Jung: The significance of the unconscious in individual education. In R.F.C. Hull (Tr.): *Collected Papers of C.G. Jung,* vol. 17, pp. 149-150. The overarching factor of introjection of experience is also seen in Erik Erikson's concept of "identity crisis" discussed in Chapter Three of this text.

[55]*Ibid.*

more and more relevance. It involves a subordination of the level-
ling devices, codes, and rules of conduct maintained in collective
education. The clue to whom shall attain toward individual education is to be found in those students—those "gifted" individuals—
who have shown resistance to collective education. On the one hand,
such students may exhibit "defects"—mental, physical, or psychological. On the other hand, giftedness may entail some special attitude
or ability, i.e., what is commonly referred to today as the "exceptional" child or person. According to Jung, such "specialness" is
usually derived from the teachings, or lack thereof, in one's home
environment.[56]

Thus, Jung's little-known views on education are intriguing for a
number of reasons. First, though his theory is very speculative and
impressionistic, it concurs to a remarkable degree with some more
descriptive findings in the current literature of moral development.
These findings, e.g., those of Kohlberg to be discussed in Chapter
Five, suggest that the large majority of human beings may not
achieve a very high level of morality throughout their lives. Con-
versely, only a small minority seems to be able to reach beyond "conventional" modes of moral thinking. Second, Jung's speculations
have even more serious implications in terms of attempting to decide
when, how, and why "individual idiosyncracies" must be blunted or
denied expression. Of course, this issue also carries with it the companion problem of deciding *whose* idiosyncratic thought and action
should be stifled and who, indeed, should be the judges in that process of determination. In a curious way, then, the highly individualistic thought of Jung might lead to another form of behavioral
engineering—or even to practices beyond the pale of controlled manipulation of human behavior.

Such dire warning signals are implicit in some of Jung's more
widely known concepts, which will now be scrutinized in light of his
so-called "typological" theory. Throughout his own life, Jung employed the Circle symbol to represent the totality of psychic life in its
basic functional components: thinking, feeling, intuition, and sensation. The first two functions, thinking and feeling, are evaluative in

---

[56]*Ibid.*, p. 151.

that they make use, respectively, of cognitive and affective judgment from the standpoint of "true-false" and "agreeable-disagreeable" discernments. The second pair of functions, intuition and sensation, are termed "irrational" by Jung because they involve simply perceptual phenomena which are irreducible to cogitative interpretation. According to Jung, each and every person predominates in certain of these functions. It is such predominance which marks the general orientation of one's personality. Regrettably, Jung gives no clear or real reasons for his typological designations beyond stating that he can "only point to the fact that this conception has shaped itself out of many years' experience."[57]

The development of psychological attitudes is related to several concepts with which Jung's name is even more widely popular: "extroversion" and "introversion." For Jung, these distinctive psychic orientations condition one's entire behavioral tone in all its manifestations. An extravert "thinks, feels, and acts in reference to . . . [external] objects."[58] That is, s/he is primarily influenced by consensual, collectively validated, social norms and codes of conduct. On the other hand, introverts relate negatively to external objects, instead relying on their own subjective experience. Consonant with his interest in balancing opposites in order to form a more total personality, Jung claims that the unconscious of each type carries on the psychic work left undone by one's consciousness. In other words, the unconscious of the extrovert is introverted, and vice-versa for the introvert.

Lurking beneath the surface of Jung's attempt at dialectical synthesis is, then, the crag-like possibility that man is fighting an uphill battle against dualisms throughout development. This cruel, harsh reality is perhaps best demonstrated in Jung's notion of the "shadow." This archetypal figure expresses the symbolic "other aspect," or "darkness," which is inseparable from totality. For Jung, the point of evil is to elucidate that which is goodness and light, to permit us

---

[57]Jung: *Psychological Types — Or The Psychology of Individuation*, H.G. Baynes (Tr.). London, Kegan Paul, 1923, p. 547. Jung's lack of reasons for his typology has not curtailed efforts to use it in modern psychological practice, particularly in career and vocational assessment; e.g., the Myers-Briggs inventory is based largely on Jung's speculations.
[58]Jung: *Modern Man in Search of a Soul*, C.F. Baynes (Tr.). London, Kegan Paul, 1933, 0. 99.

more perceptive penetration into moral enlightenment.[59] However, the shadow concept poses greater, well-nigh insurmountable, imponderables to the extent that, if Jung is correct, evil may indeed be an irreducible fact of human existence, not to be overcome lightly.[60]

To conclude our inquiry into Jung's neo-analytic contributions on a higher note, Jung does challenge us to face the critical aim of perhaps all moral life: how to emerge as an individual while maintaining harmony with the totality of life surrounding one's existence. He divides this monumental task into stages of chlidhood and adulthood in such a way that the first stage elicits knowledge of the boundaries of individuality while reserving the second stage for a more integrated understanding of how man places himself in the vastness of the Universe:

> The first half of life is spent mainly in finding out who we are, through seeing ourselves in our interaction with others . . . the realization of what we can do by ourselves, what we can do with the help of others, and what we cannot do at al. The mature [person] has discovered himself or herself as a differentiated personality spending his days and nights doing what he is fitted for by his own nature, without frittering away his energies in pointless strivings or useless regrets.[61]

The constant upshot of Jung's recommendations for child rearing is his insistence that the young person be exposed carefully and gradually to life's realities, both its good and evil sides. Too precipitate over-exposure disarms the child, leaving him unprotected and defenseless. At the same time, his/her fantasy world has already been

---

[59]Jung: *Two Essays on Analytical Psychology*, H.G. & C.F. Baynes (Tr.). London, Bailliere, 1928, p. 266. Jung's play on opposites which constantly merge is also seen in his concepts, "anima" and "animus" (male/female "soul images," or archetypes). Such dualisms have not sat well with some feminists, despite Jung's protestations that he has learned much from his patients (mostly female). See his: *Memories, Dreams, Reflections*. New York, Pantheon, 1973.

[60]See Jung: *Letters*, vol. II, R.F.C. Hull (Tr.). Princeton: Princeton U.P., 1975, p. 624: "I am strongly convinced that the evil principle prevailing in this world leads the unrecognized spiritual need into perdition, if it is not counteracted either by real religious insight or the protective wall of human community."

[61]Singer, June: *Boundaries of the Soul: The Practice of Jung's Psychology*. New York, Doubleday Anchor, 1973, pp. 277-278. Put in another way, "The first half of life is mainly dominated by the task of adaptation to the external world, implying an unfolding and expansion. In the second half of life, we are confronted with the need to discover the *meaning* of our life in particular and of life in general." Adler, Gerhard: *Studies in Analytical Psychology*, p. 138.

inhabited by ghosts and goblins — precursors of the unsafe later life that will have to be faced and dealt with in head-on fashion.[62]

Accordingly, we might summarize the implications of Jung's thought for moral development in the following manner: (1) man should be treated as an unfolding individual, slowly and relentlessly differentiating himself from the mass of humanity; (2) "every stage of life has its specific duty, and he who does not fulfill these specific duties, that is who does not live through that particular phase, has failed to experience one aspect of life, and the price of this refusal is either stultification and numbness or a neurosis";[63] and (3) man should be allowed to synthesize life in order for it to take on more holistic meaning. Thus, strong elements of stoicism, integration, and transcendence underlie Jung's psychology. They bespeak the fact that moral life is something that is expected as a natural eventuality, but one which is exceedingly difficult in its execution. In the long run, Jungian man has not only "enlightened self-interest" in morality (Freud's view), but also an obligation to the human species. This almost religious attitude forms a synthesis between oneself and the rest of human, natural, and divine existence, as in the "great penetration" of Lao-Tse. And because this task of life is so great, very few persons approach "self-actualization," i.e., the creation of a whole personality wherein one's self becomes fully defensible and indestructible.[64]

---

[62]For example, the child's learning to overcome the fear of death permits him/her to be better prepared for future lessons in life. See Adler, Gerhard: *Studies in Analytical Psychology*, p. 133: "He who tries to escape life, that is the development of his own individual personality, falls a victim to life. Only he who accepts life with all its complications and conflicts attains to full living consciousness, enabling him to find a new life-centre beyond the reach of present entanglements. Only by a full experience of life can we become conscious." In this same vein, Jung's teachings strikingly resemble those of Alfred Adler. The latter also cautions against "pampering" or "spoiling" the child on the ground that it fosters little courage in his/her struggle with reality.

[63]*Ibid.*

[64]Jung describes his idealized "self-actualized" person as one who is "excellent in knowledge" and "excellent in will," but who is "no arrogant superman." Jung: *Two Essays on Analytical Psychology*, p. 264. Nevertheless, such characterizations have not quelled the tide of criticism against Jung's evident elitist tendencies and his apparent lack of sympathy for the oppressed and persecuted who inhabit the human race. For instance, documentation of Jung's anti-Semitic leanings appears in Karier, Clarence J.: The ethics of a therapeutic man: C.G. Jung. *Psychoanalytic Review*, 63:1, 1976, 115-146.

SEARS: BEHAVIORAL CHILD REARING

Robert R. Sears is chosen as the prototypal exponent of behavioral, or social learning, approaches to the moral development of the child because he has completed perhaps the most detailed, systematic studies of how processes of moral growth are embedded in general child-rearing practices. However, from the outset, it should be understood that Sears, though largely an experimentalist rather than a clinician, was early influenced by Freud's psychoanalytic theory as well as by such learning theorists as Lewis M. Terman, Clark L. Hull, John Dollard, Neal E. Miller, Leonard W. Doob, O.H. Mowrer, and B.F. Skinner. In essence, Sears' original interest in psychoanalysis is carried with him throughout much of his mature writing on parent-child relationships and early child development, e.g., *Frustration and Aggression* (1939), *Patterns of Child Rearing* (1957), and *Identification and Child Rearing* (1965).

In Sears' model, which he calls the "directing of behavior," psychological cues and positive modeling, primarily by the mother-figure, are all-important. Indeed, it is the mother's task to provide and nurture those *impelling* kinds of stimulation which foster appropriate needs and responses in the child. Sears posits that "attractive incentives," "satisfying consequences," and "punishment for bad behavior" are necessary ingredients which impress limits, boundaries, and structured growth potential on the child's behavioral development. Much of Sears' emphasis on modeling, identification, and processes of incidental observational learning expresses how he was later influenced by the pioneering research of Albert Bandura. The kernel of Sears' ideas on these topics is contained in his *Patterns of Child Rearing*, the work most relied on in this section.

According to Sears, mothers should point out examples of (a) "good" behavior, i.e., the kind they want the child to acquire; and (b) "bad" behavior, i.e., the kind which shows the child how not to act. Thus, he finds a place for both "positive" and "negative" modeling, though the deployment of the former is generally deemed a more effective learning technique. In "positive" modeling, the mother is encouraged to use the example of figures whom the child most admires, e.g., an older brother or sister, school or neighborhood peers, fictional or public heroes, or the parents themselves. Most importantly, Sears insists that disciplinary measures in modeling training should be applied with diligent consistency.

By applying these behavioral principles, Sears is defining the learning task for the child as one of relating actions to their consequences. The mother rewards or punishes the child clearly and specifically for certain "good" or "bad" behaviors. For example, "Go to your room for hitting the baby," makes for a distinct, explicit association in the child's behavioral repertoire by which she can re-direct future misbehavior.

The means by which the child gradually applies sanctions to her behavior expresses Sears' two most important principles of moral development, both of which represent an admixture of psychoanalytic and behavioral concepts: (1) conscience and (2) identification. These concepts will be discussed at some length.

For Sears, there are three distinctive ways in which the child develops standards of self-control, or *conscience*. The first route is through purely external monitoring and intervention by adult authority figures when the child's egocentric actions impede others or do personal harm to the child herself. Second, and relatedly, the child may base self-control on fear of external punishment or anticipation of reward by those who can reinforce or withhold reinforcement. Third, the maturing child may eventually reach the point at which internal control becomes more paramount. But even at this ideal state, the child more or less comes to accept parental standards of conduct as her own. Part and parcel of this acceptance are potential feelings of guilt, shame, and self-derogation should the child countermand parental judgments. In Sears' developmental scheme, each of these progressive movements of conscience are *learned* processes which are necessary for "normal" moral growth.

Reminiscent of Bandura, Sears attempts to show how the crux of the development of conscience lies in self-instruction and the maintenance of control when either (a) no one is present to punish the child or (b) when the child is in a position free of fear or the danger of being reprimanded. In other words, if the child is able to act in a self-controlled manner in conditions of non-surveillance by external figures, Sears assumes that growth in conscience has taken place.

Though he is basically an empiricist, Sears also admits that such occurrences are difficult to observe. And, in outlining a rough timetable for the development of conscience, Sears begins from the child's second year; yet he also grants that this continuing process of cementing values and beliefs may not be thoroughly crystallized until adulthood. It is only at this mature stage that really "ethical interpretation" comes to the fore. Sears surmises, without hard and fast empirical evidence, that much of the learning of internal control is a task of the pre-pubertal years, mainly the first six to ten years of life. While not acknowledging Freud's influence in this instance, Sears maintains that these early years probably establish a threshold for how conscience will operate throughout the individual's lfe.

How might conscience be developed most effectively and endurably? Sears responds to that question through his application of the theory of *identification*. He distinguishes it from other types of learning; it is neither a process of "trial and error" nor a formal mode of step-by-step instruction, or what Sears terms "direct tuition." Instead identification occurs without specific teaching; it is an instance of that kind of "incidental," or informal, learning which sometimes appears as anathema to more orthodox behaviorists. At about age two, the child casually begins to adopt the attitudes, interests, and self-regulating sanctions of her parents. This form of social learning is closely akin to Bandura's notion of modeling and is characterized by Sears as *role practice*: observing others' actions and practicing their behavior by pretending to be those persons. Though he does not ordinarily emphasize the role of play and fantasy, it is interesting to note that Sears is compelled to rely on the use of the child's imagination to establish imitative patterns of behavior.

This imitative behavior is later transformed into adult role functions once it has been appropriately reinforced over time. Borrowing from Freud, Sears originally hypothesized that the child behaves much like her parents during the first three or four years of life, i.e., she responds to similarities between herself and her mother and these imitative actions become rewarding. Sears further employed the Freudian term "anaclitic" to describe this kind of identification. In his later writing, Sears would use another psychoanalytic concept, "defense mechanism," to characterize a secondary form of identification, "defensive identification." The latter refers to the process of internalizing the inhibiting, restricting features of the superego-figure, i.e., the parent of the same sex as the child. Sears assumes that prior anaclitic identification lays the groundwork for such secondary defensive identification. As can readily be seen, his notion relies heavily on Freud's view of superego development and the Oedipal complex.

However, the attendant matter of sex-role identification introduces perhaps the most explosive issue in Sears' entire analysis. Turning Freud's theory on its head, Sears claims that girls will normally find it easier to practice the roles and functions associated with the identification process. He presumes this to be the case because the mother is usually designated the "caretaker" figure in American culture. Whereas the little girl can mimick the mother's characteristics and be accepted for so doing, the young boy must learn to shift his attention to masculine forms of identification — even though the father figure is presumably less dominant, or at least less prevalent, in his immediate everyday environment. Thus Sears' stanch commitment to sex-typing may well reflect his matriarchal bias (as Freud had his own patriarchal prejudices), one which pervaded the 1940s, 1950s, and early 1960s during which Sears did most of his mature writing and research. One can only wonder whether Sears acknowledged watching "Father Knows Best" or "Leave It to Beaver" or whether he kept abreast of more recent admonitions which tend to soften the rigors of sex-role stereotyping.

In summary, Sears' commendable recommendations for consistent, consciously thought out child-rearing practices may now seem rather quaint and pedestrian to a society that is still reeling from the social upheaval of the later 1960s and the inward looking "cults of narcissism" of the 1970s and 1980s. In order to gauge the sense of Sears' relative unattachment from these dislocations, readers are invited to scan the chapter, "Socialization in America," in his *Frustration and Aggression*. There they will find such preachy warnings as "the teacher and the classroom rules she imposes may not be defied, and the child must not play truant." They will also be re-introduced to the same cultural characteristics which appear to perennially obsess the American psyche: aggression, competition, repression, and frustration. Sears makes no serious attempt to come to terms with wider social, political, and economic structures which may tend to sustain these dysfunctional proclivities. Particularly since Vietnam and Watergate, the moral education of the child has become even more problematic in that public heroes normally useful in modeling behavior and identification are difficult to locate. Finally, Sears' studies seem largely to reflect and reproduce the overall sampling bias of much of his research: the suburban metropolitan middle-class nuclear family.

PIAGET: COGNITIVE MORAL JUDGMENT

Possibly excepting B.F. Skinner, no psychologist has drawn as much attention during the last fifty years as Jean Piaget. The Swiss theorist's voluminous studies in genetic epistemology have made acute observations on almost every aspect of the child's development. (As will be shown, some critics are more impressed by Piaget's observational skills than they seem to be with his explanations for some peculiarly difficult concepts.)

This section treats Piaget's explicit formulation of how the child develops moral judgment. Much of Piaget's discussion on this topic is contained in his *The Moral Judgment of the Child* (1932). Later works by Piaget illustrate that his classic 1932 statement forms a consistent pattern, minor exceptions notwithstanding, with his larger theory of cognition. Given Piaget's standing in the psychological community and the fact that Kohlberg directly builds upon Piaget's theory of cognitive moral judgment, it is no accident that research on Piaget's model has been abundant. Piaget's own work and subsequent studies on his research will be considered in this section.

Piaget's stage theory assumes that cognitive and moral development proceeds hand-in-hand. He further claims that the cognitive schema and structures he describes are (a) innate; (b) invariant; (c) hierarchical; and (d) culturally universal. All these postulates are carried over into Kohlberg's research. At the same time, it is important to recognize that "children's moral judgments do not exist in a social or cultural vacuum; however spontaneous they may be in their origins, they are very much subject to direct and indirect social influences both in their rate of development and . . . in the shape they take in adulthood."[65]

Piaget's research methodology makes use of the "clinical interview" technique whereby the interviewer presents problems to the child, sees how he responds, and probes the limits of his knowledge. This method seeks to tap the child's *underlying cognitive-structural capacities*, rather than merely measure, in behavioral terms, observable surface performance. Thus there is a built-in component of speculation in Piaget's observational techniques. The clinical interview has also been called a fairly "conservative" diagnostic procedure in that the interviewer waits for the child to answer and explain *all* his responses before proceeding to more difficult operations and processes in the interview.

Not so parenthetically, the pronoun "he" is used throughout this treatment of Piaget because his study of morality included only a small sample of *male* youth, mainly from middleclass backgrounds. These children ranged in age from 5 to 13. In terms of testing moral judgment capacities, Piaget focuses on (1) how children play the game of marbles; and (2) how they respond and react to stories of moral events posed by the interviewer.

Given this research design, some critics have questioned whether Piaget is really assessing issues in moral development.[66] That is to say, Piaget seems unable to disengage implicit questions of cognitive process, particularly memory, from explicit issues in morality. Research shows that young children typically encounter difficulty in making inferences; yet Piaget's experiments require them to make inferential reference. Psychoanalytic as well as social learning theory has long recognized the problem the child faces in absorbing the relational complexities in stories. Still adults seldom consider the extreme effort at focal attention by which the child may

[65]Lickona, Thomas: Research on Piaget's theory of moral development. In Lickona (Ed.): *Moral Development and Behavior: Theory, Research, and Social Issues.* New York, Holt, Rinehart and Winston, 1976, pp. 239-240.

[66]DeVitis, Joseph L.: Cooperation and social equality in childhood: Adlerian and Piagetian lessons. *Journal of Research and Development in Education,* 17:23, 1984.

only very gradually come to assimilate and understand such complexities.[67]

In *The Moral Judgment of the Child*, Piaget details how he asks children to discriminate the "rules of the game." For example: Where do rules originate? Can they be modified? If so, when and how? How do we define lying, cheating, and "fair" punishment for transgressions? How should we distribute rewards? Should children ever contradict the authority of adults?

The latter question raises the larger philosophic discussion in Piaget's account; for a substantial portion of *Moral Judgment* is spent in a revisionist critique of Durkheim. By definition, Durkheim views education and development as the proper exercise of adult influence on "those that are not yet ready for social life."[68] Piaget intends to give greater play to the child's *own* transformations of inner perception and external reality. He implies that Durkheim has carried the traditional adult-role model of moral development to such an extent that he has been blinded to youth's potentialities:

> Durkheim thinks of children as knowing no other society than adult society or the societies created by adults (schools), so that he entirely ignores the existence of spontaneously formed children's societies, and of the facts relating to mutual respect.[69]

(Piaget's optimistic scenario of youth's spontaneity and mutual peer respect will be scrutinized later in the section.)

By contrast, Piaget's cognitive-structural approach attempts to show how sociomoral knowledge develops out of a background of authority and constraint (Durkheim) and then moves in a direction of autonomy, cooperation, and equality. In this process, Piaget posits two major stages of development:

(1) *heteronomous morality* (or *moral realism*), in which the very young child bases his moral judgment on unilateral respect for authority figures, i.e., "objective" rules of parents and other adults. This stage primarily reflects a *morality of constraint, absolutistic* thought patterns,

---

[67]Schachtel, Ernest: Focal attention. In Coser, Rose (Ed.): *The Family: Its Structure and Functions.* New York, St. Martin's, 1969, p. 389.

[68]Durkheim, Emile: *Education and Sociology* (1922), S.D. Fox (Tr.). Glencoe, Free Press, 1956, p. 71.

[69]Piaget, Jean: *The Moral Judgment of the Child* (1932), Marjorie Gabain (Tr.). New York, Collier, 1962, pp. 343, 356.

and only "immanent" concepts of "fairness" and "justice."

(2) *autonomous morality* (or a *morality of equity and cooperation*), in which the young person, by middle childhood to early adolescence, begins to develop a more "subjective" sense of autonomy and reciprocity. In this stage, social experience, principally peer interaction, becomes the main vehicle for increasingly cooperative, egalitarian growth.

Piaget claims that the young child's immature cognitive processes are severely inhibited by a lengthy period of *egocentrism*. He uses this term descriptively, not pejoratively, to characterize the relative inability to separate components of internal and external reality. In practical terms, egocentrism prevents the child from *decentering*, or placing himself in the viewpoint of another person. Thus Piaget postulates that maturation beyond egocentrism marks the beginning of all morality. It should also be noted that some recent studies on children's communication skills indicate that the child may not be so typically "egocentric" as Piaget would lead us to believe.[70]

Once the child resolves some of the difficulties inherent in distinguishing his own "reality" from the givens in external reality, Piaget foresees a more or less natural process of gradually unfolding moral development (much in the manner of Rousseau's "ripe tomato" analogy). Unless one is somehow deprived of social experiences, particularly with peers, Piaget assumes that such growth will occur. To a significant extent (perhaps more than any other theorist), Piaget argues that *peer interaction* is vital because it is the only legitimately *equal* form of moral participation. As such, he implies, on a broader level, that equality may likewise be the most legitimate testing ground for morality in general. Like Adler, Piaget also characterizes cooperations as the defining standard for both a "mature" culture and personality:

> One may conceive of cooperation as constituting the ideal form of equilibrium towards which society tends when compulsory conformity comes to break down . . . . Cooperation . . . seems to be essentially the social relation which tends to eliminate infantile phenomena . . . .

[70]Donaldson, Margaret: *Children's Minds*. New York, Norton, 1978, pp. 11-25. Also: see Maratsos, Michael: Non-egocentric communication abilities in preschool children. *Child Development*, 44:697-700, 1973; and Lloyd, Peter: Communication in preschool children. Unpublished doctoral dissertation, Edinburgh University, 1975.

[It] is the limit and norm of every human group that has ever come into being.[71]

Nevertheless, the interactional "give-and-take" which Piaget extolls as the *sine qua non* of an "autonomous" and democratically-based morality has not been conclusively substantiated in the research literature. Bronfenbrenner observes that peer interaction in American youth leads to excessive dependence on peer approval.[72] Thus the maturing child may simply be relinquishing one form of authority for another, i.e., adult authority gives way to peer authority. Lickona has evaluated the effect of both peer interaction and the absence of adult constraint and finds mixed results:

> The evidence is strongest for the role of cognitive development, mixed but generally supportive regarding the contribution of peer experience, and weakest with respect to the role of freedom from the constraining influence of adult authority.[73]

More generally, Rosen cautions against extrapolation from Piaget's experiments since they revolve solely around the boundaries and limitations of "stories" and the "game of marbles" paradigm.[74] Though the child may appear to be gaining autonomy in certain areas of rule experience, he may well remain heteronomous in rule applications in other areas of life.

Meanwhile, Epstein has challenged Piaget's position on the ground that young children may not adequately understand the difference between "breaking" and "changing" a rule.[75] Epstein's experiments indicate that once a child is aware of the distinction, s/he is more likely to permit modifications in the rules of the game.

In its story-telling technique, Piaget's experiments often pair stories: one story tests whether the child recognizes moral *intentions* in the story characters, and the other story attempts to show whether

---

[71]Piaget, Jean: *The Moral Judgment of the Child*, pp. 346, 348, 371.

[72]Bronfenbrenner, Urie: *Two Worlds of Childhood: U.S. and U.S.S.R.* New York, Sage Foundation, 1970. Also: see Hogan, Robert: Moral conduct and moral character: a psychological perspective. *Psychological Bulletin*, 79:227, 1973.

[73]Lickona, Thomas. Research on Piaget's theory of moral development, p. 240.

[74]Rosen, Hugh: *The Development of Sociomoral Knowledge: A Cognitive-Structural Approach.* New York, Columbia U.P., 1980, p. 35.

[75]Epstein, R.: The development of children's conceptions of rules in the years four to eight. Unpublished senior paper, University of Chicago, 1965.

the child can foresee *consequences* in the story development. Once again, Piaget seems to have "built in" a contaminating element in his own experimentation. In effect, he imposes "either/or" choices on the child (one for "intentions," the other for "consequences"), thus appearing to steer him in certain directions. There is also a larger question as to whether the concepts "intention" and "consequences" can be so neatly distinguished. Finally, in cognitive developmental terms, it may be that assimilation of intention and consequences proceeds at differing rates for the very same child under experimentation. In other words, the cognitive acquisition of each process may not follow in precise or proximate tandem.

Another monumental problem in applying Piagetian research is concerned with Piaget's equation of cognitive and moral ability. (Kohlberg, of course, makes the same equation.) Piaget himself frowned upon standardized intelligence testing, arguing that it did not tap the child's underlying conceptual capacities. Accordingly, on Piaget's own terms, conventional IQ tests would be inadequate measures by which to assess any presumed correlation between intelligence and morality.

The human and social dangers implicit in such equations and measurements (or, more accurately, mismeasurements) have engendered exceedingly inhumane social practices, e.g., sterilization of prostitutes and the so-called "feeble-minded," as in the case of the Human Betterment Foundation and the California legislature in the early 1900s.[76] That movement was led by such psychologists as Lewis Terman and David Starr Jordan of Stanford.

Other issues also leave the curious student of moral development with some open-ended questions about possible *alternative explanations* for Piaget's findings. May growth in morality have more to do with *experiental* influences than with logical or intellectual abilities *per se*? Might children fare better in experimentation on morality if they were more *familiar* with the *tasks* involved in such evaluation? In a related sense, do *perceptual* factors and *attentional* problems inherent in the arrangement of these tasks confuse the child and therefore yield a distorted picture of his actual capabilities? Are Piaget's explanations

---

[76]Karier, Clarence J.: Testing for order and control in the corporate liberal state. *Educational Theory*, 22:154-180, 1972.

adequate proof for the existence of inborn cognitive schemas and structures which supposedly form the basis for evolving moral development? And does such development necessarily imply simultaneous growth in moral and cognitive judgment and action?

More positively, Piaget has at least grounded his theory of morality in *semi-observational* techniques, however limited his focus on stories and the game of marbles leaves his investigation. This is in stark contrast to Freud, Adler, and Jung, who tend to spawn their notions in airier forms of speculation. Moreover, Piaget has afforded penetrating vision for disparate schools of psychology from psychoanalytic theory, through social learning theory, to current models of cognitive structuralism. As an example, the "game of marbles" analogue generates a host of questions and issues for rule theory.[77] Piaget's descriptions and conceptualizations also help explain the construction of civilization and its attendant norms, roles, and exceptions.[78] It goes without saying that social learning theory has long been interested in rule application and modeling behavior. Cognitive-structural research in moral development might well provide richer perspectives for distinguishing how rules emerge and what constitutes appropriate modeling behavior. And, in the end, Piaget conjures up perhaps the most intriguing question of all: Might a plane of *equality* be the most compelling crucible by which to assess moral judgment in its purest form?

Gruber and Vonèche conclude their analysis of Piaget's theory of moral development on an equally sobering note:

> Piaget is aware of a deep social question raised by his work. Although moral judgment develops in certain regular ways, it is by no means obvious that adult behavior lives up to the idealized norms of which children are capable. There are various plausible ways of understanding this disparity. For example, it may be that all mature adults are capable of high levels of moral judgment, but not necessarily of moral behavior, given the pressures of an often irrational and corrosive society. Or, it may be that living in such a world eventually erodes the capacity for moral judgment and even for rational thought.[79]

---

[77]Szasz, Thomas: *The Myth of Mental Illness.* New York, Hoeber-Harper, 1961.

[78]Bettelheim, Bruno: Education and the reality principle. In Bettelheim: *Surviving and Other Essays.* New York, Vintage, 1980, p. 138.

[79]Gruber, Howard E. and Vonèche, J. Jacques (Ed.): *The Essential Piaget.* New York, Basic, 1977, p. 155. For another extensive, clear account of Piaget's theory, see: Kay, William: *Moral Development: A Psychological Study of Moral Growth from Childhood to Adolescence.* London: Allen and Unwin, 1970.

CHAPTER THREE

MORAL DEVELOPMENT IN ADOLESCENCE

HAVIGHURST: DEVELOPMENTAL TASKS

DEVELOPMENTAL tasks is a concept that was first discussed as early as 1935, was used by Erik Erikson, and culminated in a major study by Robert J. Havighurst.[1] Here Havighurst's approach to the concept will be presented.

A developmental task emerges at a certain period in an individual's life, "successful achievement of which leads to happiness and to success with later tasks, while failure leads to unhappiness in the individual, disapproval by the society, and difficulty with later tasks."[2] Developmental tasks have been formulated for infancy and early childhood, middle chidhood, adolescence, early adulthood, middle age, and later maturity. Our focus will be on the adolescent period and, specifically, moral development. Though the developmental tasks differ, once understood how they function in adolescence their functions in other stages are analogous. Listed below are developmental tasks for adolescence.

1. Achieving new and more mature relations with age-mates of both sexes
2. Achieving a masculine or feminine social role
3. Accepting one's physique and using the body effectively
4. Achieving emotional independence of parents and other adults

---

[1]Havighurst, Robert J.: *Human Development and Education*. New York, McKay, 1953.
[2]*Ibid.*, p. 2.

53

5. Achieving assurance of economic independence
6. Selecting and preparing for an occupation
7. Preparing for marriage and family life
8. Developing intellectual skills and concepts necessary for civic competence
9. Desiring and achieving socially responsible behavior
10. Acquiring a set of values and an ethical system as a guide to behavior

Of the above tasks, the last two relate directly to moral development in adolescence. The notion behind this and other tasks is that they need to be achieved at the proper time to be achieved well, and the failure in one task can cause partial or complete failure in subsequent tasks. Consequently, it is important for adults to provide the conditions to facilitate appropriate task achievement.

A critical task of adolescence is to develop a mature set of values and desirable traits that would characterize the good person and the good citizen. This is a lengthy process that begins in early childhood with the emergence of conscience.

In order to fulfill the task of desiring and achieving socially responsible behavior, it is necessary to take account of society's values so that one can participate as an effective citizen in the community. To achieve this task, there are psychological and cultural bases for doing so but no biological ones. In other words, this is learned, rather than inherited, behavior that stems from society's influence upon the individual.

In terms of the psychological basis, the adolescent learns to make sacrifices for a greater good of the group, family, or community and, in turn, may be rewarded for manifesting the desired behavior. Various ceremonies, national holidays, and rituals, whether patriotic or religious, ranging from Independence Day to religious communion, help cement social bonds. Youths during late adolescence become strongly altruistic and are willing to consider the larger social good.

The cultural basis of this task can be viewed in relation to different social classes. Among the middle class, many youths may leave their local community to attend college or in search of employment and do not develop strong ties with their community. In contrast, the upper class teach their offspring the responsibility of social service, even though these teachings fail conspicuously to be absorbed by some. The lower class youth feels less responsibility to the community and relates more closely to neighbors or to an extended family structure.

To better promote this developmental task, secondary schools can teach about the life of the local community through studies of its various social, economic, and cultural features. Some appreciation for one's region and nation can be gained by reading history and biography. Ceremonies can also be used to inculcate greater loyalty to the community and nation. Additionally, youth could be encouraged to devote two or three hours daily to community work.

The other adolescent task in moral development is to acquire a set of values and an ethical system as a guide to behavior. Thus the task involves formulating a set of values capable of being realized and consciously to strive to achieve these values. This also involves keeping one's values in harmony with one's view of the world.

Havighurst holds that values form a hierarchy, and that the primary sources of all values are physiological drive. These drives—for food, warmth, physical activity, bodily stimulation—are patterned values for the infant from which other values are derived. These derived values reside in the infant's striving to gain the mother's approval and alter other adults: hence, the child learns to defer, when necessary, satisfaction of the patterned values in order to gain the deferred values. The adolescent learns desired values, according to this approach, in six ways: satisfaction of physiological drives, fulfillment of emotional experiences, consistent rewards and punishments, association of the desired value with love or approval, inculcation by an authority figure, reasoning and reflective thinking.

To help the adolescent acquire values one should recognize the role of identification and imitation and, consequently, the use of biography can be an influential source of value formation. Since youth learn desirable and undesirable values from peers, some adult supervision of these activities is needed. The study of values can be pursued through philosophy, literature, history, and art; secondary students also need to examine the scientific world view in relation to values. Not to be overlooked are ceremonies that bring youth together for an experience that offers emotional satisfaction.

Assessment of Developmental Tasks

Several hypotheses were tested, rating scales devised, and the reliability of ratings assessed.[3] It was hypothesized that good achievement on a developmental task at one age would be followed by good achievement on similar tasks at a later age; that good achievement on a developmental task is associated with good achievement on tasks at the same age; and that in a minority of cases good achievement on one task may be used to compensate for inadequate achievement on other tasks; and that there are certain personality characteristics significantly related to achieving these tasks.

The procedures used were to select five developmental tasks for study (one task was the development of conscience, morality, and a set of values); then definitions were developed of success and failure in achieving these tasks, and rating scales were devised. Reliability of ratings among the eight judges was determined by computing product-moment correlation coefficients (a basic formula for calculating the coefficient of correlation betwen two variables), and it was found that the average ratings of any one set of four judges had nearly the same reliability as the average of the other set of judges.

The development of conscience, morality, and a set of values was found to be rather highly related to other tasks.[4] The lowest relationship was found between emotional independence and other tasks. Another hypothesis confirmed that good performance on a task at one age is followed by good performance on this and similar tasks at a later age. The one exception is the task of learning appropriate sex roles. Considerable fluctuation in task performance occurs between the ages of 10 and 13; consequently, relationships are closer on task performance between ages 13 and 16 than ages 10 and 13. The hypothesis that some persons use good achievement in one task to compensate for inadequate achievement in another was not confirmed. As for personality traits, some were consistently related to task achievement. Those traits significantly related to the development of conscience, morality, and values for both males and females are

---

[3]*Ibid.*, ch. 19.
[4]*Ibid.*, ch. 20. Also see: Peck, Robert F., et al.: *The Psychology of Character Development.* New York, Wiley, 1960, ch. 7.

realistic assignment of responsibility or behavior of self and others, realistic balance self-perception, and outer emotional stability.

What are the advantages and shortcomings of developmental tasks? This approach may be of help to teachers in planning objectives and a guide for parents as to what can be expected from their offspring at different developmental stages. It shows that even while human development is an individual matter, certain tasks are common to all. And it is an effective way of organizing fragmented knowledge — physical maturation, drives, motivation, emotion, and socialization. It also emphasizes the importance of timing and pacing of effort to relate activities and resources meaningfully to the appropriate developmental tasks.

One conceptual problem is that developmental tasks are said to lead to happiness when achieved and to unhappiness when failure occurs. "Happiness," however, is a weasel word that not only varies in meaning from one culture to another but within a culture according to social class, ethnicity, religiosity, and one's philosophy of life. It may be easier to talk about unhappiness than happiness, as certain noxious conditions — unrelieved pain, a terminal illness, death of loved ones, abject poverty — are likely to cause most anyone unhappiness. Yet, even here, one can choose one's attitude toward personal misfortune, as Viktor Frankl did while incarcerated in a Nazi concentration camp.[5] Thus if developmental tasks as a concept is to be more scientifically testable, terms such as "happiness" and "unhappiness" need to be deleted and unequivocal, operational terms substituted.

While the concept of developmental tasks moves away from an individualistic needs approach and gains balance by relating the growing individual to social expectations, the task of "desiring and achieving socially responsible behavior" seems to make the group or the community the standard of behavior. This is true of some other tasks as well (e.g., the task of developing civic competence). Havighurst, especially in his examples, seems to assume that the task is what the law requires or what the community accepts. But this raises problems for youth who are reared in bigoted communi-

---

[5]Frankl, Viktor: *Man's Search for Meaning.* New York, Washington Square Press, 1963.

ties where discrimination and injustice are widespread. Thus implicit in the tasks is compliance with authority, not one of the highest moral levels (as we shall see in chapter five when Kohlberg's developmental stages are presented).

The stages may also illustrate certain cultural or social class biases. One adolescent task is to prepare for marriage and family life. Yet increasingly many adolescents and young adults are choosing to remain single. Another task is that of selecting and preparing for an occupation. This task, however, is not one that upper class youths must fulfill either because of economic necessity or upper class expectations; in other words, they usually have a choice whether to prepare for a career.

The developmental tasks are not merely descriptive but are normative as well: they prescribe what the individual ought to do at each stage in order to become happy and successful. But some nations and cultures will define the tasks differently. Nazi Germany and Stalinist Russia define the task of "desiring and achieving socially responsible behavior" strikingly different than Western democracies. But adolescents growing up in those two nations, once they conform to Nazism or Stalinism, have fulfilled the developmental task as well as youth who learn the ways of Western democracies. Thus, in this respect, the developmental tasks are an inadequate moral guide.

Havighurst's approach to the developmental tasks is to prescribe that schools should take considerable responsibility in helping the young to attain them. But what he has done is to assume a progressive stance so that those who hold different educational philosophies or theories (e.g., essentialism, perennialism, etc.) would refuse to countenance these tasks. In other words, those who believe that schools should aim only to develop cognitive abilities and not the whole person could not accept developmental tasks as formulated by Havighurst, who spends much time outlining the school's role in promoting these tasks.[6] Of course if all but the cognitive tasks are turned over to the home and other institutions and agencies, then those of other philosophical persuasions may possibly take more interest in this developmental theory.

---

[6]Havighurst: *Human Development and Education*, chs. 6, 8, 12-15.

ERIKSON: IDENTITY CRISIS AND IDEOLOGY

Erik H. Erikson is widely known for a variety of notable intellectual achievements. His psychosocial theory of development most distinctively places ego psychology in the context of socio-cultural perspectives. And his uniquely sensitive and penetrating psychohistorical analyses of such legendary figures as Gandhi and Luther have been singularly applauded. However, this section of the text will deal more directly with Erikson's theoretical contributions to the generation of ethics and morality in adolescence. Accordingly, we will focus on certain key aspects of Erikson's "Eight Stages of Man," or "life cycle," primarily Stage Five which refers to the endemic polarization involved in solving the tortuous problems of "identity" and "identity confusion." These appear to be peculiarly crucial tasks of adolescent moral development.

In his modification of Freud's theory of psychosexual development, Erikson attempts to utilize the broad resources of religion, anthropology, and other cross-cultural interdisciplinary studies. In a very real sense, he seeks to view the subjectivity of the individual with respect to larger social milieu, both cultural and transgenerational. Erikson's deeply moving, almost poetic, exposition takes on the substance of a hopeful utopian voyage in an age strewn with strife and seemingly dangerously unhinged from reliable direction.

Once again, we appear to be confronting those same dilemmas posed in Durkheim's original paradigm. It is Erikson's personal as well as scholarly mission to provide a more inclusive, universal ethical vision as opposed to the largely relativistic stance adopted by Durkheim.

According to Erikson, each individual is faced with, and must reconcile, certain recurrent fundamental problems, or conflicts, at each stage of life. These conflicts and their respective focal stages are not to be viewed as tightly compartmentalized passages in Erikson's typological scheme, i.e., there may well be overlapping in the chronology and duration of the stages. However, unless problems in each successive stage are solved, the individual may well be riddled by prior unresolved conflict throughout life. The following synopsis outlines Erikson's eight stages and the presenting problem polarities at each stage (for the sake of comparison, Freud's psychosexual stages are listed in parentheses):

1. Trust vs. mistrust (oral)
2. Autonomy vs. shame and doubt (anal)
3. Initiatie vs. guilt (genital)
4. Industry vs. inferiority (latency)
5. Identity vs. role diffusion (adolescence)
6. Intimacy vs. isolation (young adulthood)
7. Generativity vs. stagnation (middle adulthood)
8. Ego integrity vs. despair (late adulthood)

For Erikson, the adolescent's particular battle over identity and role diffusion is perhaps the most perplexing crisis in one's life (or at least it appears that way for struggling youth who have lived through that typically tumultuous period). Moreover, in our contemporary culture, Erikson insists that this struggle is even more pronounced and vexing: "The patient of today suffers most under the problem of what he should believe in and who he should — or, indeed, might — be or become; while the patient of early psychoanalysis suffered most under inhibitions which prevented him from being what and who he thought he knew he was."[7]

In adolescence, the maturing individual is confronted with the following confusing, conflictual identity polarizations which Erikson maintains must be balanced if s/he is to sustain epigenetic growth:

(a) Time perspective vs. time diffusion
(b) Self-certainty vs. identity consciousness
(c) Role experimentation vs. negative identity
(d) Anticipation of achievement vs. work paralysis
(e) Sexual identity vs. bisexual diffusion
(f) Leadership polarization vs. authority diffusion
(g) Ideological polarization vs. diffusion of ideals[8]

Once one considers the myriad changes facing the adolescent at this stage of development, the reasons for the inevitability of "iden-

---

[7]Erikson, Erik H.: *Childhood and Society*, 2nd ed. New York, Norton, 1963, p. 279.
[8]Erikson, Erik H.: Identity and the life cycle: Selected papers. In *Psychological Issues* (Monogr.). New York, International Universities, 1959, p. I:1.

tity crisis" and role confusion become clearly evident. Physiological and libidinal changes make youth feel threatened by those same peers whom they increasingly seek out for recognition — at the very time that ego and superego processes are also becoming intensified. There is a concurrent tendency to identify with "heroic" figures, to wage war in some romantic ideological cause, to belong to a social group at all costs: "What the individual has learned to see in himself must now coincide with the expectations and recognitions which others bestow on him."[9] Nor have career choice and the mastery of intellectual and affective competencies been fully articulated or accomplished. Finally, there is a compelling need to balance the "sameness and continuities" of one's past with a less defined, more unsettling future in which one cannot be certain of one's aims or the likely routes for their achievement.

To quote one of Erikson's aphorisms about the perils of the adolescent's plight: "I ain't what I ought to be, I ain't what I'm going to be, but I ain't what I was."[10] Thus the underlying goal of adolescence is to harmonize one's past and future through a fuller integration of ego identity.

Yet these efforts do not always meet with instantaneous harmony or sucessful adaptation. Sometimes youth, as in the case of the Beatniks of the 1950s or the Hippies of the 1960s, opt to rebel against past identities, seeing themselves as outside the restrictive codes of conduct promulgated by adult authorities. Such youth may embody what Erikson terms *negative identity*, i.e., "a desperate attempt at regaining some mastery in a situation in which available positive identity elements cancel each other out."[11] However, any attempt to establish identity, even "negative" identity, is better than having no identity at all. In this regard, for example, Erikson speaks in sympathetic tones of Black Muslim and Black Power advocates who seek to surmount conditions of "inaudibility, invisibility, namelessness, facelessness."[12]

---

[9]Erikson, Erik H.: *Insight and Responsibility: Lectures on the Ethical Implications of Psychoanalytic Insight.* New York, Norton, 1964, p. 90.
[10]Erikson, Erik H.: In M.J.E. Senn (Ed.): *Symposium on the Healthy Personality.* New York, Macy Foundation, 1950, p. 139.
[11]Erikson, Erik H.: The problem of ego identity. *Journal of the American Psychoanalytic Association,* 4:88, 1956.
[12]Erikson, Erik H.: *Identity: Youth and Crisis.* New York, Norton, 1968, pp. 25-27.

Some relief from the traumatic experiences of adolescence is provided by what Erikson sees as a *moratorium* period — a psychosocial, culturally accepted delay of adulthood which is somewhat analogous to Freud's concept of latency, i.e., a protective release from quickened libidinal interest. In American culture, extended forms of education, military service, and living at home with one's parents afford outlets for such a moratorium. (Of course, this moratorium may also be welcomed by the culture as a "benevolent" way to "cool off the economy," that is, keeping students out of the labor market.) In any case, this "safety valve" allows youth to step back from more active confusion, to take some perspective, and to partake of "provocative playfulness" in socially sanctioned ways.

The special fashion in which adolescents typically invest their energies is articulated in Erikson's use of the concepts *ideology* and *fidelity*. Erikson characterizes ideology as "a systematized set of ideas and ideals which unifies the striving for psychosocial identity in the coming generation, and it remains a stratum in every man's imagery, whether it remains a 'way of life' or becomes a militant 'official' ideology."[13] In this confusing attempt to establish a set of values and beliefs, Erikson insists that adolescents adopt a particular kind of moral virtue, i.e., *fidelity*, or "the ability to sustain loyalties freely pledged in spite of the inevitable contradictions of value systems."[14] Fidelity serves to "confirm" ideologies, and Erikson contends that the force of affiliation with one's peers is as important in this confirmation as any "truth" in the ideology. (Except for Piaget, no other theorist than Erikson focuses so acutely on the role of peer interaction in establishing and maintaining value systems.)

The prevalence of ideology in adolescence is a form of *ritualization*, a concept which is also vital to any understanding of Erikson's description of the evolution of morals and ethics. "Ritualization" denotes those ceremonial habits of everyday behavior which allow humans to lead balanced, adaptive lives while being affirmed by their fellows. In adolescence the ritualization of ideology customarily

[13]Erikson, Erik H.: Psychosocial identity. In *International Encyclopedia of the Social Sciences*, vol. VII. New York, Macmillan, 1968, p. 63.
[14]Erikson, Erik H.: *Insight and Responsibility*, p. 125.

becomes transformed into a *totalism*, a zealous devotion to "black-and-white" standards of right and wrong in the name of some fanatical ideal. Of course, Erikson postulates that this circumstance is a fairly natural event which tends to balance out during the course of one's life cycle.

At this point it seems appropriate to show how Erikson distinguishes "morals" from "ethics." The former term is more akin to "infantile morality" or "adolescent ideology;" whereas the latter term is synonymous with a "letting go" of puerile values which harbor any semblance of righteousness, prejudice, or similar kinds of moralism.[15] For Erikson, a more "mature" and "universal" form of ethics disavows moralistic fanaticism of any sort because, in his words, "you can always be sure that the loudest moralists have made deals with their own consciences."[16] In essence, Erikson divides the task of ethical development into three distinct realms: (1) *moral learning* in childhood; (2) *ideological experimentation* in adolescence; and (3) *ethical consolidation* in adulthood.[17]

Erikson also provides an impressionistic thumbnail sketch of various sub-species of morality: (a) a *premoral* position is equated with a denial of any need for morality; (b) an *amoral* position "flaunts accepted norms"; (c) an *antimoral* position "militantly negates all authority"; and (d) an *anti-authoritarian*, yet moralistic, position "condemns the adult world with righteous fervor."[18] Needless to say, Erikson is searching for a more all-encompassing, universalistic morality than any of those listed above.

Erikson's most mature delineation of the ethical realm is couched in "a universal sense of values assented to."[19] His analysis tends to base itself in the bedrock values common to all the great major religions of the world. In particular, it is largely quilted from the Judeo-Christian faith in the Golden Rule: "love thy neighbor as thyself."

---

[15]Erikson, Erik H.: *Identity: Youth and Crisis*, pp. 119-120; 259-260.

[16]Erikson, Erik H.: *Life History and the Historical Moment*. New York, Norton, 1975, p. 22. See also Erikson, Erik H.: *Dimensions of a New Identity: The 1973 Jefferson Lectures in the Humanities*. New York, Norton, 1974, pp. 108, 114-117.

[17]Erikson, Erik H.: *Life History and the Historical Moment*, p. 206.

[18]Erikson, Erik H.: Reflections on the dissent of contemporary youth. *Daedalus*, 99:165, Winter, 1970.

[19]Erikson, Erik H.: *Life History and the Historical Moment*, p. 207.

Erikson reformulates this rule in accordance with his notion of *mu-tuality*, in which devotion to the other reconciles "the antagonisms inherent in divided function."[20] That is to say, Erikson admonishes that "what is hateful to yourself, do not to your fellow man."[21] In the final analysis, then, Erikson's ideal form of ethical action would produce "mutuality between the doer and the other."[22] Such a vision is reminiscent of the moral programs of Gandhi and Martin Luther King, Jr. Thus, for Erikson, as for Adler, personal growth and communal change are of one piece; and the crisis of identity cannot be artificially separated from historical development and commitment among generations past, present, and future.

Nevertheless, Erikson's almost messianic call for universalism has often run up against harsher barriers in actual human history. Countless social groups, classes, religions, and nations have practiced what Erikson terms a *pseudo-species mentality*. The bearers of ideological sovereignty are typically consumed with false pride and an unquenchable belief in the power and immortality of their group's ideas and ideals. From the Inquisition to Nazi Germany and Jonestown, such world views have been known to lead to destruction, bloody tragedy, and unfulfilled hopes. For example, it may be no coincidence that most wars have been fought in the name of nationalism or religious intent.

These realistic considerations tend to leave Erikson's well-intentioned effort to articulate clinical psychological observation in a sort of moralistic, exhortative vacuum of its own. Erikson would like to claim that he grounds his ethical stance not "on the moral injunction of avoiding affront to the ideal but on the ethical capacity to provide strength in the actual."[23] Yet Erikson, like Adler, is also guilty of a form of naturalistic fallacy in his own argumentation. As Paul Roazen, perhaps Erikson's most perceptive critic, puts it: "The problem is that Erikson does not seem sufficiently aware of the logical dilemma in moving from empirical statements to value judg-

---

[20]Erikson, Erik H.: *Identity: Youth and Crisis*, p. 219.
[21]Erikson, Erik H.: *Insight and Responsibility*, p. 243.
[22]Erikson, Erik H.: The golden rule and the cycle of life. In White, Robert (Ed.): *The Study of Lives: Essays in Honor of Henry A. Murray.* New York, Atherton, 1963, p. 423.
[23]Erikson, Erik H.: *Insight and Responsibility*, p. 177.

ments, in inferring an 'ought' from an 'is.' [24]

Implicit in Roazen's critique is a more grievous gap in Erikson's own utopian agenda: the serious neglect of policy recommendations to implement social and institutional change. In many ways, Erikson's soothing ego psychology amounts to an adjustment psychology which might serve to cushion men's acceptance of the status quo. In the end, using his own poetical language, Erikson's ideology may thus be seen as a credo brightly shining in the night—but one which is disabled in the deployment of powerful social and political rudders.

---

[24]Roazen, Paul: *Erik H. Erikson: The Power and Limits of a Vision.* New York, Free, 1976, p. 119. Roazen's analysis is especially helpful in applying social critique to Erikson's treatment of morality. For a more sympathetic view of Erikson, see Wright, J. Eugene, Jr.: *Erikson: Identity and Religion.* New York, Seabury, 1982. Recently, feminist criticism has been less sympathetic to Erikson's controversial notion of "inner space," which posits that female personality development is confined by the "groundplan" of the womb. See Okin, Susan Moller: *Women in Western Political Thought,* Princeton, Princeton U.P., 1980, pp. 238-241.

CHAPTER FOUR

MORAL DEVELOPMENT AND HIGHER EDUCATION

THE college years make lasting impressions upon many students—friendships formed, social life enjoyed, studies pursued, memorable professors, and growth in maturity and understanding. But what specific effect does the college experience have upon the student's values and moral development? ("College" refers throughout to the undergraduate years, whether in a college or university.) Does it merely reinforce and stabilize the values of entering freshmen, or does it bring about lasting value changes of a certain type? Does the college experience lead to growth in moral development, or is moral development similar to what early psychologists regarded about I.Q. scores—that the maximum potential is reached by age sixteen? What theories would best help to explain moral development among this age group?

Thus this chapter focuses on different theories of moral development in the college years and the body of data-based research about how higher education affects or does not affect moral development. Among those surveyed are such diverse thinkers and researchers as Philip E. Jacob, Arthur Chickering, William Perry, Douglas Heath, Roy Heath, and Kenneth Keniston.

JACOB: VALUE CHANGE AND CURRICULUM

A pivotal point of heightened interest in the impact of college on student values occurred with the Jacob study.[1] This study's controversial findings led subsequent researchers to seek to confirm or refute them. The study was conducted to discover the effects of general education in the social sciences on the values of American college students. Jacob reviewed several hundred studies since 1920, visited 30 institutions, and gathered evaluative data on courses and curriculum at these and other institutions.

He found the values of the American college student "remarkably homogeneous" and the students themselves "gloriously contented," "unabashedly self-centered," and "politically irresponsible." Traditional moral values are held by most students although, as in the case of academic dishonesty, they do not always feel bound by them. Students are dutiful toward citizenship responsibilities insofar as they expect to obey laws, pay taxes, and vote, but are largely "politically illiterate." Students predict another major war within a dozen years but give little attention to international affairs. The above profile would be characteristic of 75-80 percent of American college students surveyed.

The principle effect of a college education is to bring about a general acceptance of a shared body of attitudes and standards from the college experience. More consistency in values among students can be discerned among seniors than freshmen. Thus the overall effect is to socialize the student and refine his or her values. College is a selective process to begin with, as many who have divergent attitudes do not attend and those who find the experience uncongenial drop out (up to 50 percent at the time of the study).

One of the most significant features is that student values did not substantially change as a result of the curriculum, whether enrolled in a conventional liberal arts program, an integrated general education curriculum, or a professional-vocational program. Even when the curriculum was redesigned to confront students with personal and social value issues, it rarely engendered a significant difference in beliefs, much less in their conduct.

Moreover, the quality of teaching has little effect on value outcomes in general education. The effect of the good teacher is indis-

[1]Jacob, Philip E.: *Changing Values in College.* New York; Harper, 1957.

tinguishable from the poor one in terms of influence on values. Nor does it make much difference what teaching method is employed, though students become more involved and concerned when they are asked to confront value issues and make decisions.[2] Although students alter their opinions on many issues and become more tolerant of those with different views, college has a socializing rather than a liberalizing effect on values. "The values with which they arrive and which are integral elements of their personality, are still there when most students leave."[3]

Jacob examined a wide range of research, but the studies' conclusions have been lumped together even though the studies use diverse methods, differently formulated problems, and were conducted by researchers of different abilities. Moreover, he gives no greater weight to important longitudinal studies than to simple comparisons between students exposed or not exposed to a human relations course. Nor does Jacob explore the number of professors who firmly believe that academic life should serve strictly intellectual purposes and who have no interest in values other than those embodied in their own discipline.

In the decade following the Jacob study (published in 1957), a voluminous literature appeared based on seeking answers to more specific and more complex questions. Researchers sought to determine the learning conditions, types of students, and the specific ways students changed. This meant looking at the college's public image, institutional size, the college environment, and other variables that interact with one another. Twelve years after the Jacob study Feldman and Newcomb concluded, after an examination of four decades of research studies, that "there are conditions under which colleges have had (and, we assume, will continue to have) impacts upon their students, and not least upon students' values. Moreover, the consequences of these impacts often persist after the college years."[4]

---

[2] *Ibid.*, ch. 1.
[3] *Ibid.*, p. 53.
[4] Feldman, Kenneth A. and Newcomb, Theodore M.: *The Impact of College on Students.* San Francisco, Jossey-Bass, 1969, vol. 1, p. 4.

CHICKERING: EDUCATION AND INTEGRITY

Arthur W. Chickering has sought to synthesize research and theory in higher education in order to develop a conceptual framework faithful to the findings and relevant to a wide variety of decisions.[5] To accomplish these tasks, he has described seven vectors or major dimensions of development during the college years — competence, emotions, autonomy, identity, interpersonal relationships, purpose, and integrity. He relates these vectors to six major aspects of the college environment: objectives; institutional size; curriculum, teaching, and evaluation; residence hall arrangements; faculty and administration; friends, groups, and student culture.

Our interest lies primarily with the vector of "developing integrity" because it pertains to values and standards; however, a brief statement about the other vectors will help clarify Chickering's framework. The vector of "developing competence" concerns intellectual, physical and manual skills, and social and interpersonal relationships. Underlying one's ability to develop competence in these areas is confidence in problem-solving and ability to achieve one's goals.

"Managing emotions," a second vector, is a task not completed by the end of secondary school, especially with problems of aggression, sexuality, and attitudes toward authority of home and community. One task is to lessen repression of the earlier years, learn to accept early feelings as legitimate emotions, gain greater self-awareness, flexible control, and freedom of expression.

"Becoming autonomous" means to become emotionally independent and instrumentally independent. The former means that one becomes free of the constant need for reassurance and approval; the latter refers to the ability to solve problems independently and remain flexible in relation to one's desires and needs.

These previous three vectors help one in the process of "establishing identity." Here the individual discovers those experiences that establish a rhythm so that self-destructive patterns are avoided; it also concerns the clarification of various aspects of ourselves — from the physical to the interpersonal. A sense of identity helps promote change in other vectors of development.

---

[5]Chickering, Arthur W.: *Education and Identity.* San Francisco, Jossey-Bass, 1969.

"Freeing interpersonal relationships" means to develop greater tolerance for a diversity of human behavior, increased ability to relate to others as persons rather than stereotypes. Here there is also a shift away from dependence upon close friends to interdependence.

The developmental vector of "clarifying purpose" involves seriously raising and attempting to answer such questions as "Who am I?" "What am I going to be?" "Where am I going?" One needs to deal with these questions in three areas: recreational and avocational interests, vocational plans and aspirations, and general life-style considerations. By developing purpose, the individual is able to integrate these three areas and thereby imbue one's life with greater meaning.

Returning to the vector of "developing integrity," it is related to establishing identity and clarifying purposes because one strives for an internally consistent set of beliefs and values that guide behavior. Most researchers indicate a change toward increased liberalism during the college years; the changes usually involve not so much relinquishing one value for another as that of gradually modifying the values brought to college. Thus college may more likely affect the basis for holding values, how they are held, and the role they play in one's life. Chickering insists that it is more important for values to have a larger role in the student's life than to change the content of values. The tasks are to humanize and personalize values and develop congruence among them.

Carrying out these tasks involves developing objective analyses of different conditions and learning to estimate the consequences of various alternatives. Religious values developed in the home may also come under scrutiny. By humanizing values they may become relative to differing circumstances which, in turn, may generate anxiety and a search for deeper moorings and commitment. Integrity arises when the inconsistencies between belief and deed become minimal so that once the ramifications of a situation are grasped, the response is determined. But achieving congruence is a lifelong task and the individual will need to develop new sources of strength as his support system of friends changes and new relations are formed.

Chickering explores six college environmental conditions or variables that make a difference in student development (these conditions were mentioned earlier). While all of these conditions or variables have the potential to influence student development, Chickering cites residence hall arrangements and faculty-student interaction as having an especially important impact upon values.

Friendships in residence halls are first established by propinquity and the architectural arrangement of living units. Experiences with roommates and friends help reduce ethnocentrism and promote greater acceptance of others. These changes for students are not always easy: placed in a position where one must learn to live with others and in which others could hardly be ignored, accommodation is learned, followed gradually by tolerance and acceptance of others. But as enrollment increases or institutions become more selective in admissions, opportunities for a genuine residential community may be diminished. Yet these changing conditions do not diminish the need for more lasting social relations, which are necessary to provide a sense of identity and emotional support in everyday life.

Chickering recommends that residential units become reference groups for their members whereby they convey meaningful norms and standards. This goal can best be accomplished by permitting students to live in the same unit as long as they desire; keep the size of the unit small enough so that each individual can have some impact on the whole; let students choose their own living space within the unit; and provide each residence unit operating funds for which they will be held accountable at the end of each semester.[6]

Students need both models and anti-models to develop their values. They need a distinctive college environment, professors with strong value commitments, and personal value experiences which can be integrated with their educational development. The anti-models are those whom students actively reject — the tyrant, the crowd-pleaser, haranguer, and others. The characteristics of faculty that help students to develop not only competence but purpose and values are accessibility, professors with well-integrated values, professors knowedgeable not only of their discipline but of student developmental problems, and the ability to converse with and listen effectively to students.[7]

What, then, can be said of Chickering's approach to moral development by way of summary and assessment? Chickering, by use of

---

[6]*Ibid.*, ch. 11.
[7]*Ibid.*, pp. 241-252.

vectors and environmental influences, has provided a framework to embrace multiple and complex developmental characteristics. He has sought to envision the student as a total person engaged in an educational process that can significantly influence development; these processes range from classroom experiences to resident hall interactions. The breadth of his framework provides a panoramic view of complex variables without resort to reductionism.

The developmental vectors, however, do not all seem to be on the same plane. Some appear to be tasks, others are more similar to outcomes; in other words, some are processes and others are achievements. "Developing competence," "managing the emotions," and "freeing interpersonal relationships" are processes or tasks, but "becoming autonomous" or "establishing identity" are achievements that may occur as one gains skill in the processes. Establishing identity and becoming autonomous are not entirely completed at any stage of development; the other vectors would appear to be instrumental to them.

Is the term "integrity" a felicitous one for describing value development? It is misleading should the reader associate it with a character trait approach in which integrity is only one of many different character traits identified but not sufficient to embrace them all. For instance, such an approach, in addition to integrity, may talk about such traits as honesty, loyalty, reliability, self-control, conscientiousness, benevolence, and the like.

Evidently what Chickering means is that integrity refers to the ability to organize values into internally consistent patterns to guide action, and the development of congruence between espoused values and conduct. This is an important aspect of value development but not the only important one. Other important abilities are the capacities to think through one's values, to analyze and critically appraise them so that they may be either reformulated or else, if accepted largely unchanged, one could provide adequate grounds for doing so.

Perhaps part of the problem lies in Chickering's definition of values: "Values are standards by which behavior is evaluated."[8] Stan-

---

[8]*Ibid.*, p. 123.

dards, however, are only one among several types of value expression; moreover, values are not restricted in their functions to evaluating behavior. Value statements also take the form of rules (e.g.: "Persons who smoke or drink will be denied membership.") and principles (the Golden Rule, which is actually a principle, and Kant's categorical imperative, one version of which says to "So act that the maxim of your will could always hold at the same time as a principle establishing universal law."). Values are also used to develop normative ethical systems (Epicureanism, Stoicism, Christian ethics, Kantian ethics, Utilitarianism).

Values are not limited to the evaluation of behavior, as they are integral to aesthetics and also take the form of utility values. Thus values are used to appraise a work of art (e.g.: symmetry, harmony, color, texture, design, expressiveness, etc.). Utility values are used to appraise consumer products such as a new car (mileage per gallon, resale value, warranty, initial costs, spaciousness, etc.).

Chickering holds that "The proper function of colleges is to increase the role of values in the lives of students — not to modify the content of values held."[9] But certainly this claim cannot be made for church-related colleges that enroll irreligious students. Moreover, the claim seems inconsistent with Chickering's own position that colleges should develop salient, consistent institutional objectives that pervade college life and are taken seriously by both faculty and students. Different patterns of institutional objectives can be discerned in some colleges.[10] What happens to a student, for instance, who comes from a home where he was taught to accept values on faith or authority and matriculates at a college that has as one of its objectives the promotion of critical thinking in all aspects of life? Obviously something will have to change in the student's value system if the college's faculty and students take institutional objectives seriously. Thus, Chickering's views notwithstanding, where institutional objectives are seriously pursued and a distinctive ambience and esprit de corps animates the college, value change will occur. As noted earlier in the Feldman and Newcomb review of research studies, value change does occur and it often persists after graduation.

---

[9] *Ibid.*, p. 226.
[10] *Ibid.*, ch. 8.

PERRY AND HEATH: GROWTH, COMMITMENT, AND MATURITY

Perry's longitudinal study of value development during the college years shows students moving from an early belief in authority's omniscience to relativism and finally to commitment, except for those students who suspend or reverse the process of growth.[11] Although his data are limited to the college setting and a single college (Harvard College), he believes it has wider implications for understanding late adolescence in a pluralistic society. By reviewing examination questions in large sections of freshman courses at Harvard College from 1900 to 1960, a shift can be discerned from seeking information and correct answers to a relativist stance, which was defined as considering questions in more than one frame of reference. In addition, Harvard has become increasingly diverse in its student body: 45 percent of its students in 1900 came from outside Massachusetts; in 1960, 72 percent. The significance of these changes is that students will confront a more relativistic, pluralistic environment that may seriously challenge their entering values.

A Checklist of Educational Views (CLEV) was devised to identify students in terms of certain desired dimensions; the CLEV was then administered to a random sample of 313 freshmen and, on the basis of their scores, invitations were sent to 55 students, 31 of whom accepted. Tape-recorded interviews were made in May and June each year, including 17 complete four-year records. Later the study was extended to obtain a larger sample of students' report of their four years in college, to articulate a developmental scheme found in the reports, and to test the scheme's validity. The researchers were able to show that the scheme of development could be identified in all the students' reports sampled.[12] In the study a *developmental pattern* was conceived as "an orderly progress in which more complex forms are created by the differentiation and reintegration of earlier, simple forms," and *growth* was defined simply as "progress in development."[13]

---

[11]Perry, William G.: *Forms of Intellectual and Ethical Development in the College Years: A Scheme.* New York, Holt, Rinehart and Winston, 1970.
[12]*Ibid.*, ch. 1.
[13]*Ibid.*, p. 44.

Perry observed three major value development stages: the modifying of dualism; the realizing of relativism; and the evolving of commitments. The line of development is in the order listed (dualism the early stage and commitments as the final stage). In each stage three positions were observed, consisting of a total of nine.

In terms of the dualistic stage, the child views his family and the outside world in position 1 according to in-group vs. outgroup. Morality consists of obedience to authority, with authority sometimes considered omniscient. Educational tasks are conceived in terms of memorization and hard work. Only three or four freshmen in the study were found at this position.

In Position 2 the student revolts against heterogeneity and, consequently, rejects critical thinking. Diversity and complexity are viewed as alien to him. But in Position 3 uncertainty and complexity are not considered obstacles generated by authority but existing independently. Here the student begins to question hard work in class as a basis for standards.

Positions 4 through 6 mark the emergence of relativism. The student perceives authority, in Position 4, as wanting him to think relativistically; he is still tied to what he believes authority wants him to do. By the time the student has reached Position 5, the dualistic structure of authority and the outside world has collapsed and knowledge is increasingly viewed as contextual and relativistic. This change comes about when it is seen that dualism cannot assimilate relativism. The student, in Position 6, apprehends the need for personal choice in a relativistic world; commitment is now viewed as the resolution of relativism, but it has yet to be experienced.

The last three positions move the student into the stage of commitment. Position 7 describes the student who has decided on his responsibility in some major area of his life, as in strongly stating a career decision. In Position 8 the student has developed a style for pursuing his commitment; finally, a person develops a sense of "who he is," both in content and style, in Position 9.

For Perry, growth is a moral issue insofar as the individual exhibits will, effort, and courage. A person who has moved to one of the higher positions is a "better" person. Courage is involved because one is faced with redefining and extending responsibilities in confronting increased uncertainty and complexity.

Perry claims that his study holds assumptions found in contextualistic pragmatism, post-Wittgensteinian Forms of Life, and existentialism as it refers to personal commitment. But it is not self-evident that such influences undergird the study unless the reader is first apprised of them and told to search for them.

Perry generalizes to other student populations from his limited sample. He also assumes that development from dualism to relativism to commitment is an advancement both intellectually and morally. Though it is obvious that the dualistic position has irremediable weaknesses, the weaknesses of the other stages are generally overlooked by Perry. Value relativism is unable to explain how one can show that another value position is wrong, as those values, which may be in opposition to one's own, may relate to a different context and social conditions. For instance, though a relativist may disapprove of infanticide, in a different culture that accepts the practice because of high birth rates, insufficient food, and the like, the relativist cannot say that this practice in the other culture is wrong.

Commitment, the highest stage, is also open to question. Sometimes commitment is not chosen by the individual but derived from what is "socially acceptable in our group." It is not uncommon for an individual to fear being committed to a career or a way of life that lacks the approval of one's group. The mere existence of commitment provides no clue in itself as to its derivation. Another difficulty with commitment is that it may lead not to openness but to dogmatism, fanaticism, and truculent opposition to all who hold differing positions.[14] What is needed is to guard against commitments that are not reflectively developed and not always open to further scrutiny, against those that become inflexible and dogmatic. It is therefore important to know how a commitment was reached and how it is presently held.

Despite these misgivings, Perry's study has shown distinctly how development continues during the college years, the characteristic changes in development, and the way that these changes affect the

---

[14]See Hoffer, Eric: *The True Believer.* New York, Harper, 1951.

thought and values of undergraduates. Teachers who use this schema to identify their students' stage of development could re-shape their instruction to coincide with the students' present stage in order to communicate and evaluate more effectively.

A different approach to growth and development in the under-graduate years is through the use of personality typologies. From a stratified sample of 625 liberal arts candidates at Princeton, Roy Heath picked 36 entering freshmen for whom he would serve as aca-demic counselor and meet with individually once a week and serve in small group discussion during their undergraduate years.[15] He matched this group with a similar control group. Through the modes of verbal behavior exhibited in interviews, Heath searched for a framework to explain observed differences. He initially devel-oped scales for recording students' satisfaction in academic work and friendship; he also constructed a third scale to rate self-understanding and acceptance. Comparative growth of students was represented by a triangle and each student was classified as low, me-dial, or high. After typologies were developed, students were classi-fied from low to high within the framework of their respective typology.

He found four different personality types: non-committers, hus-tlers, plungers, and reasonable adventurers. The non-committers avoid involvement, trouble, and appearing ridiculous. They hold a myth about themselves: that they could do many important things if they went all-out; since they could go all-out if desired, they want the freedom to bide their time. Actually, to go all-out poses a terrify-ing risk because it could refute the myth, and the non-committers are paralyzed by the fear of appearing ridiculous and impotent.

In contrast, hustlers thrive on activity, deal with conflicts aggres-sively, and have a strong need for achievement. They are keenly competitive and frequently insensitive to others' feelings despite a desire for acceptance. Hustlers are restless, constantly devising plans and seeking activities that will help them attain their goals. They tend to overintellectualize their motives and not be attuned to their inner feelings. Life, for them, is a battle; consequently, one must

---

[15]Heath, Roy: *The Reasonable Adventurer*. Pittsburgh, University of Pittsburgh Press, 1964.

look out for himself. They prefer courses that emphasize logic and factual material rather than those that concern aesthetic appreciation and subjective judgment. Thus hustlers are strong-willed persons with much control over their deeper impulses. This means eschewing introspection and solitude for the opportunity to be with others, even though these relations are superficial. Hustlers lack warmth and originality; they maintain inordinately high standards for themselves in order to overcome fears about their inner weaknesses, which they do not want to confront openly. Most of the hustlers are mesomorphs: they have a muscular, athletic physique.

On the other hand, the plungers push ahead and overextend themselves; they act in spurts, enthusiastically taking up a project and suddenly laying it aside as their interest wanes. They cope with their anxieties by conveying them to anyone willing to listen. Students in the project who took up acting were plungers, presumably because they had already played in life some of their stage roles. Their quest was also a search for identity and an integrating philosophy to bring their lives greater coherence.

The ideal type is the reasonable adventurers. These students alternate effectively between involvement and detachment, curiosity and criticalness; whereas less effective personalities show tendencies predominantly toward one pole. Their friendhsips are based not so much on shared experiences as their ability to convey deeper feelings. The reasonable adventurers, more than the other types, were capable of tolerating ambiguity by suspending judgment.

Reasonable adventurers have many projected projects; their attitudes differ from the dilettante's because they are better integrated and have more depth. They have a lively sense of humor that is rarely at others' expense. And though their intellectual endowment may be no more than average, they use it exceptionally well. They are, in other words, fully-functioning persons.

In terms of growth during the undergraduate years, most all the students in the sample grew except for six instances where there was some slippage in the junior year. The hustlers grew the least of the different types. Heath found that non-committers were stimulated to grow by moderate challenges and inner life activators. Non-committers evidenced disconnected personalities and needed to reunite the inner fantasy world with the outer social world. These inner life activators were formed in prose and poetry that stressed the theme of contradiction in human nature (as found in such writers as Donne, Dostoevsky, Eliot, Emerson, Kierkegaard, and others). As a result of these experiences, non-committers became more assertive and self-expressive.

In contrast, significant change in hustlers seem to come only through a calamity, such as unexpected failure to achieve any of one's most important goals devised for the college years. One alternative to a crisis as a means of breaking the hustlers' rigid superstructure is to place them in marathon social sessions with peers where their facade can eventually be melted through love and affection. Once they see that they are liked for their own sake, they can begin to shed their pseudoself.

The plungers, on the other hand, are strong individualists and need someone to understand their wide mood swings. They can grow more rapidly surrounded by understanding friends and teachers. But any gains made may be transitory unless they can appropriate a philosophical framework and make it their own, one which will integrate their inner self.

Seven students were classified as reasonable adventurers in the original sample; this number increased to sixteen or 45 percent of the original sample. Heath's sample, as compared to the control group, received more academic and non-academic honors.

What are the educational implications of this study? Heath believes that reasonable adventurers are needed among the student body to provide a healthy academic atmosphere. He also thinks that four years of liberal arts study, though perhaps not even enough, should be maintained and any moves to reduce the curriculum to two years of general education should be resisted. The humanities proved especially important for the non-committers, and the writing of essays in literature classes, when handled carefully by the instructor, enabled hustlers to directly encounter their alien inner selves and prepare the groundwork for change. The senior thesis is extolled by Heath because, as a major undertaking, the completion of it brought students greater self-respect.

One thing that became evident was that no single method of

teaching, advising, or counseling proved effective for all students. What is effective varies with the student's temperament and level of development. Nondirective counseling is suited to medial level non-committers but useless for a medial plunger. Heath predicts that one will be in a better position to decide how best to use test scores when in the reasonably near future personality measures and developmental levels are included in college orientation testing programs.

In evaluating Heath's study, he has provided a new intellectual handle for interpreting the diversity among undergraduates. By constructing four personality types from his lengthy observations and interactions, he has offered a different but convenient and intelligible way of understanding different growth patterns and growth impediments. His study also underscores the need for devising different instructional and advising procedures depending upon the type of student. The typologies redefine growth by relating growth patterns to the respective goals of the different personality types, even though the ultimate goal is to facilitate the emergence of additional reasonable adventurers.

Heath's recourse to Sheldon's classification of body types when discussing hustlers overlooks cultural influences. In other words, hustlers are not necessarily the way they are because of somatype but because the larger culture has certain expectations about young men with muscular physiques and tends to push them into athletics and other assertive activites; consequently, after the fact, strong drive and assertiveness comes to be associated with mesomorphs.

The grounds for extolling a liberal arts curriculum are tentative when it is remembered that only the humanities were singled out (although Heath erroneously included fine arts with the humanities) for promoting personality change. Since the social sciences and natural sciences are part and parcel of a liberal arts curriculum, the majority of the curriculum did not have any identifiable effect on personality change. Thus Heath needs to modify his statement about the value of the liberal arts on personal development. Moreover, he does not have an alternate curriculum with which to compare the Princeton undergraduate program, and it may be that a different curriculum would be equally or more effective.

Typologies may be considered classificatory schemes that represent shorthand ways of helping us understand complex phenomena; yet typologies may also overgeneralize and obscure needed distinctions. It is difficult to believe that all undergraduates fit neatly into one of these four typologies rather than having some significant traits characteristic of two or more types. Another problem with these typologies is that they do not appear to be amenable to empirical testing; other researchers need to see whether his study can be replicated.

Another problem is that the derivation of the personality types from the larger culture is not clearly shown. What the reader needs to see are the social and cultural influences that shape personality types rather than treating personality as *sui generis*. Each culture tends to value certain types and discourage and punish other types. Historically, the Spartans valued the militaristic type, the Christian Middle Ages elevated priestly functions to an ultimate level, the Renaissance extolled the universal man, nineteenth century Romantics sought the natural man unfettered by society's corruptions, and today the Soviet Union seeks to shape the communist citizen, while the United States extolls capitalistic virtues of ambition, drive and accumulating wealth. Thus typologies are limited as an explanatory tool not only because they overgeneralize and thereby fail to make needed distinctions but also because they are culturally and temporally relative constructs.

A different approach to student development in college was pursued by Douglas Heath through the concept of maturity.[16] The first study's themes are What is a mature person? and How does a mature person adapt to disturbing information? The mature person, he found, manifests five traits: increases stability of organization so that one's identity can be maintained over time, seeks new information which is then made congruent with his self-organization, becomes progressively organized by internalizing social reality (allocentric) rather than need-dominated (autocentric), able increas-

---

[16]Heath, Douglas H., with the assistance of Heath, Harriet E.: *Explorations of Maturity: Studies of Mature and Immature College Men.* New York, Appleton-Century-Crofts, 1965; and Heath, Douglas H.: *Growing Up In College: Liberal Education and Maturity.* San Francisco, Jossey-Bass, 1968.

ingly to symbolically represent and coordinate more of his external and internal worlds, and becomes more autonomous for his decisions and actions.

The self, he claims, is composed of schemata, skills and valuators. The schema is a structure of internal psychic elements; the skill is an ability to cope with the environment; and the valuator consists of beliefs, interests, and preferences that serve as a basis of judgment and action.

Three samples were evaluated on a number of psychological measures (including Rorschach and MMPI). A panel of 18 judges (including nine students as well as faculty members) rated 24 Haverford upperclassmen. On several tests better organized students were able to analyze, conceptualize, and judge disturbing information more accurately and efficiently. The ability to recover from the disturbing information and to perform adaptively was positively related to MMPI Ego-strength scale.

His second book reports research studies over a ten-year period with various groups of Haverford College students: freshmen, sophomores, seniors, recent graduates, and other alumni. A number of research techniques were employed: standardized psychological tests, Self-image Questionnaire and the Perceived Self-questionnaire developed by Heath, and recorded standardized interviews.

Heath, once again, sought to assess changes in Haverford students in terms of what it means to mature (maturity is defined in terms of the characteristics stated above.) He notes four structures that define the person: intellectual growth, establishment of guiding values, increasing knowledge about oneself, and the development of social and interpersonal skills. By combining these four structures with the five characteristics of maturity generates 20 hypotheses concerning how a person grows.

The investigation involved 73 randomly selected subjects; comparisons with nonparticipants in the study showed few differences. Analysis of the data provided a large number of statistically significant correlations. In terms of the principal developmental changes, the seniors were more mature than freshmen and may have matured beyond where they themselves were as freshmen. The rate of maturing varied in different sectors of the personality. Maturing in autonomy and in personal relations was more frequently discerned than in symbolization.

Heath also evaluated alumni and found somewhat different effects of college than from students presently enrolled. Maturing of one's values became more significant for alumni and one's interpersonal relations less significant. The maturing effects of college are a more stabilized, integrated self-concept.

In these studies Heath has sensitively observed changes in development, and he makes important contributions to our thinking about psychological health. His conceptual framework is able to formulate hypotheses with a high level of generality, and the studies skillfuly integrate theoretical and empirical approaches.

Generalizations, however, must be limited from the Haverford student population because it is a small, highly selective residential college. Heath's personality variables are a set of assumptions rather than a theory, and more precisely stated hypotheses need to be drawn. He is actually studying psychological health rather than maturity, as the latter concept can more plausibly be defined in terms of assuming responsibility in appropriate social roles and adapting successfully to adult norms—traits which may not necessarily have a high correlation with psychological health. Though Heath has important ideas to convey, his presentation is frequently repetitious and diffuse. In dealing with students' ethical motives, he should have observed actual life crises. Finally, the studies need replication in a different setting by another researcher.

KENISTON: UNCOMMITTED AND DISSIDENT YOUTH

Kenneth Keniston has been a keen observer during the 1960s and early 1970s of uncommitted and dissident youth. In Keniston's study of the uncommitted, he takes up two themes: one theme is based on three years of research with uncommitted students at Harvard College; the other theme focuses on an analysis of the maladies and failures of technological society.[17] (Only the first theme will be discussed.)

In identifying uncommitted students, subjects were interviewed

---

[17]Keniston, Kenneth: *The Uncommitted: Alienated Youth in American Society.* New York, Harcourt, Brace & World, 1965.

and given the Thematic Apperception Test. Symptoms of alienation discerned include pessimism, resentment, distrust, anxiety, egocentricity, sense of being an outsider, and rejection of happiness as a goal. Those scoring high on indices were classified as alienated; low, classified as conformists; and another group of 12 were classified as "extremely non-alienated," and those of average classification as "not extreme either way."

Alienated youth studied were passionately interested in intellectual and aesthetic activities, enjoyed verbal disputes, professed agnosticism, and evinced a distrust of human nature and all ideologies. These young men rejected conventional American values, especially occupational and family roles. Instead they restlessly searched for adventure and new experiences; they have a rich fantasy life and yearn for fusion or loss of selfhood. They were too alienated to become beatniks (which involves accepting an identity, some solidarity) and were not politically active.

Their characteristics, as uncovered by Keniston in intensive clinical interviews with 12 Harvard men, were an identification with their mothers, who were described as highly sensitive, frustrated, aesthetic women; while their fathers depicted their sons as having failed to realize their fathers' aspirations for them. These youth also evinced a revulsion toward the values of conventional youth culture and the educational system. The major themes in their lives, says Keniston, are but extreme reactions that affect all youth.

Keniston has illuminated the lives of uncommitted youth. He does not present in any detail, however, the methodology which generated the data. The reader also is not given a portrait of the two other control groups. Specific alienation problems were combined rather than separated (e.g., alienation of youth, alienation of intellectuals, alienation based on marginal psychological characteristics and traumas).

Keniston's study of radical youth involved interviews with 17 youths who participated in "Vietnam Summer," a movement in opposition to America's activities in Southeast Asia.[18] This is a study in political socialization.

---

[18]Keniston, Kenneth: *Young Radicals: Notes on Committed Youth*. New York: Harcourt, Brace, & World, 1968.

These youths came from affluent homes where parents treated them with directness and humanity; parents permitted their views to be criticized. But they still identified with parents selectively by imitating those qualities they perceived as valuable and opposing other qualities. The young radicals retained a set of core values concerning relationships, motives, and feelings but rejected the political philosophies and institutions that systematized them.

Kenniston found previous explanations inadequate: the young radical was neither a "radical rebel" (a rejection of authority derived from rejection of authority of one's family) nor a "red-diaper baby" (radicalism learned from one's radical parents).

Instead he postulates the "stage of youth," a stage that intervenes between adolescence and adulthood that arose as society freed youth from the need to work while concurrently demanding more formal education. Keniston does not regard his subjects' radicalism as a neurotic defense mechanism but as a natural and integrated part of their life experiences.

Postmodern youth may not face in their parents a gap between preaching and practice any greater than previous generations; yet because of rapid social changes and parental ambivalence between early values of their own childhood and those of their adulthood, they are unable to rationalize the discrepancy between creed and deed. Today's youth, therefore, may be able to perceive this discrepancy better than earlier youth.

Keniston has also brought together 20 essays; all but two have been published before.[19] Some essays seem fragmentary and incomplete; his earlier essays, which contain typologies later abandoned, lead the reader to question why he included these selections. This dichotomy between uncommitted and radicals forces many different youth styles into these categories even though most youth do not fit into either one. Keniston's studies do not include women and non-whites; he especially overlooked a significant opportunity to study the black protest movement of the 1960s.

Despite these misgivings, his studies have traced dissent from the Civil Rights sit-ins and the Berkeley Free Speech movement. Kenis-

---

[19]Keniston, Kenneth: *Youth and Dissent: The Rise of a New Opposition*. New York, Harcourt Brace Jovanovich, 1971.

ton perceives the youth rebellion as international in scope, a combination of a new psychological stage and peculiar historical conditions. Thus he finds that the college experience promotes more complex, individuated persons whose presence in a confused and rapidly changing society stimulates the emergence of counter-cultures.

In summary, it has been shown that many fruitful theories of moral development in the undergraduate years have advanced our understanding and laid to rest the findings of the Jacob study; thus the college experience can have a significant influence on moral and personal development and bring about value change. These changes continue after college according to Douglas Heath's study of 68 male college graduates in their thirties who had become more mature on all of the general measures of maturity used in the study.[20] Thus, as Withey observed, college may be the last important opportunity for a self-confronting experience. "It provides an opportunity of meeting people of varying backgrounds with different ideas, at a time of life when self-examination is maximized and in an institution that legitimizes the identity task of exploring and reevaluating one's values and ideologies."[21]

[20]Heath, Dougleas R.: What the enduring effects of higher education tell us about a liberal education. *Journal of Higher Education*, 47:173-190, March-April, 1976.
[21]Withey, S.B.: *A Degree and What Else? Correlates and Consequences of a College Education.* New York, McGraw-Hill, 1971, p. 39.

CHAPTER FIVE

MORAL DEVELOPMENT THROUGH
THE LIFE SPAN

KOHLBERG: COGNITIVE MORAL DEVELOPMENT THEORY

LAWRENCE Kohlberg and his associates have conducted research over the past several decades on a cognitive moral development theory, and the theory has been an object of considerable attention and debate within the international academic community. His theory was influenced by Dewey's psychological writings,[1] and also is indebted to Piaget's pioneering work.[2]

Kohlberg has sought to overcome the deficiencies of Piaget's research by using a much larger sample that is more broadly based socially and is composed of equal proportions of popular and socially isolated children. He is also concerned with the principle of justice rather than, as with Piaget, simple virtues and vices and such concepts as cooperation and equity.

Rather than relative values, Kohlberg's findings show culturally universal stages of moral development. His theory, he claims, is both psychological and philosophical, and his findings generate a philoso-

---

[1]However, Kohlberg's universal ethical values, along with other aspects of his theory, differ from Dewey's views, which are transactional and situational.

[2]For Kohlberg's early development of his theory, along with his criticisms of Piaget, see his: Development of moral character and moral ideology. In Hoffman, M.L. and Hoffman, L.W. (Eds.): *Review of Child Development Research*. New York, Russell Sage Foundation, 1964, vol. I, pp. 383-431; Stage and sequence: The cognitive development approach to socialization. In Goslin, D.A. (Ed.): *Handbook of Socialization Theory and Research*. Chicago, Rand McNally, 1969, pp. 347-480.

phy of moral education designed to stimulate moral development rather than teach fixed moral rules. Kohlberg believes that a philosophic concept of morality and moral development is required, that moral development passes through invariant qualitative stages, and that moral development is stimulated by promoting thinking and problem-solving.

Kohlberg's study yielded six developmental stages allotted to three moral levels. Subsequent retesting of the groups at three-year intervals has shown growth proceeding through the same stages in the same order.

I. *Preconventional Level*

Stage 1: Orientation to punishment, obedience, and physical and material power. Rules are obeyed to avoid punishment.

Stage 2: Naive instrumental hedonistic orientation. The child conforms to obtain rewards.

II. *Conventional Level*

Stage 3: "Good boy" orientation designed to win approval and maintain expectations of one's immediate group. The child conforms to avoid disapproval. One earns approval by being "nice."

Stage 4: Orientation to authority, law, and duty, to maintain a fixed order, whether social or religious. Right behavior consists of doing one's duty and abiding by the social order.

III. *Postconventional, Autonomous, or Principled Level*

Stage 5: Social contract orientation, in which duties are defined in terms contract and the respect of others' rights. Emphasis is upon equality and mutual obligation within a democratic order. There is an awareness of relativism of personal values and the use of procedural rules in reaching consensus.

Stage 6: The morality of individual princples of conscience that have logical comprehensiveness and universality. Rightness of acts is determined by conscience in accord with ethical principles that appeal to comprehensiveness, universality, and consistency. These principles are not concrete (like the Ten Commandments) but general and abstract (like the Golden Rule, the categorical imperative).

These stages are based on ways of thinking about moral matters. Stages 1 and 2 are characteristic of young children; whereas Stages 3 and 4, according to Kohlberg, are ones at which most of the adult population operates. No more than 20 to 25 percent of the adult population have reached the last two stages, with only about 5 to 10 percent at Stage 6.

However, after failing to find Stage 6 subjects in Turkey, Kohlberg reduced the number of stages to five by making Stage 6 an advanced Stage 5 form.[3] Kohlberg also postulated the existence of a Stage 7 that involves contemplative experience of a nonegoistic and nondualistic variety.[4] But since no empirical evidence of this stage has been found, and since Stage 6 has been abandoned, Stage 7 can also be discarded from his theory.

Kohlberg insists that schools have been teaching a "bag of virtues" — a particular set of values and character traits that are culturally relative.[5] These virtues range from Aristotle's choice of temperance, liberality, pride, good temper, truthfulness, and justice to the well known Boy Scout bag. These and other virtues are instilled by exhortation, example, and practice.

In his objection to the bag of virtues approach, Kohlberg cites the landmark Character Education Inquiry in the 1920s.[6] The vast majority of pupils, on the basis of tests administered, acted honestly in some situations and dishonestly in others, and there was consistency

[3]Kohlberg, Lawrence: Revisions in the theory and practice of moral development. In Damon, William (Ed.): *Moral Development*. San Francisco: Jossey-Bass, 1978, pp. 83-87.

[4]Kohlberg, Lawrence: Stages and aging in moral development — some speculations. *The Gerontologist*, 13:497-502, 1973.

[5]Kohlberg, Lawrence: Education for justice: A modern statement of the Platonic view. In Sizer, Theodore R. and Sizer, Nancy F.: *Moral Education: Five Lectures*. Cambridge, Mass., Harvard University Press, 1970.

[6]Hartshorne, Hugh and May, M.A.: *Studies in the Nature of Character: Studies in Deceit* (Vol. I), Studies in Service and Self-Control (Vol. II), Studies in Organization of Character (Vol. III). New York, Macmillan, 1928-30.

in these patterns when the tests were repeated. It was concluded that behavior is highly specific, depending upon the particular case; there is no such thing as honest and dishonest children but only honest and dishonest acts. Thus little evidence was found of unified character traits or generality in moral behavior.

Kohlberg offers several other objections to this approach.[7] Arbitrariness exists in composing the list of virtues, depending upon the composition of committees to develop such a list, their agreements and inconsistencies. Virtue words are relative to cultural standards that are psychologically vague and ethically relative (e.g., the inability to agree on the meaning of "self-discipline"). Moreover, by labelling a set of behaviors with a positive or negative trait does not in itself show that it is of ethical importance but represents an appeal to social conventions. Additionally, longitudinal research findings raise doubts whether childhood personality traits are stable or predictive over time and stages of development. Childhood traits, as used in Head Start, are not predictive of positive or negative adjustment. Research suggests that various character traits do not stand for consistent personality traits but are merely evaluative labels.[8]

Returning to the stages of development, Kohlberg contends that the stages are "structured wholes," or organized systems of thought. Stages imply qualitatively different modes of thinking. Second, stages form an invariant sequence. Third, stages are "hierarchical integrations."[10]

Stages are defined according to responses to moral dilemmas classified in terms of a scoring scheme. Validating studies include a twenty-five year study of fifty Chicago-area boys, middle and working class; a six-year study of Turkish village and city boys of the same age; and various cross-sectional studies in Britain, Canada, India, Israel, Honduras, Taiwan, and Yucatan.

Stages are organized systems of thought, as about 67 percent of most subjects' thinking is at a single stage irrespective of which moral dilemma is used to test it. The typology is referred to as

---

[7]Kohlberg, Lawrence: Development as the aim of education: The Dewey view. *Harvard Educational Review*, 42, no. 4:449-496, 1972.

[8]Kohlberg: Education for justice, pp. 69-70.

[10]Kohlberg: Stage and sequence.

"stages" because they represent invariant developmental sequences: all movement is forward and does not omit steps, the stages arise one at a time and in the same order, even though children move through the stages at varying speeds. The stages are hierarchical insofar as thinking at a higher stage comprehends within it thinking at lower stages. Individuals prefer the highest stage available to them in their thinking because higher stages can more adequately organize the multiplicity of data, interests, and possibilities open to each person. Thus the higher stages are not only more socially adaptive but are philosophically superior because they move the individual closer to basing moral decisions upon a concept of justice (Stage 6). This is the level of principles which can be universalized (i.e., applied to all persons everywhere), where the individual views moral judgment not from his or her individual perspective or society's values, but from the perspective of any human being. Thus, following Kant, Stage 6 universalizes moral principles.

Both Kohlberg and Piaget are structuralists. Kohlberg states that Piaget's theory is *structured* because it abstracts a form of thinking or structure from the *function* which the thinking is serving.[11] The same function (moral judgment) is served by successive structures of judgment which displace or reintegrate prior structures for serving this purpose. In contrast, Kohlberg claims that Erikson's theory is functional because it defines stages not by structures but by new functions of the self, person, or ego.

In keeping with the structuralism of Kohlberg's theory, the moral stages are considered *structures* of moral judgment as opposed to the *content* of moral judgment. As an example, in one of the moral dilemmas an issue is raised whether the husband of a dying woman should steal a drug if the seller refuses to reduce his price and the husband cannot raise the money to afford to purchase it. Whether or not to steal the drug is the content of the moral judgment in the situation; reasoning about the choice defines the structure of the moral judgment. The individual's structure of moral judgment is embodied in what he or she defines as valuable in the moral issues raised, and the

---

[11]Kohlberg, Lawrence: Continuities in childhood and adult moral development revisited. In Baltes, P. and Schaie, K.W. (Eds.): *Life-span Developmental Psychology.* New York, Academic Press, 1973.

reasons given for holding the value(s). Thus in Stage 1, for instance, life is valued for power or possessions; whereas only in Stages 5 and 6 is life viewed as inherently worthwhile, apart from other considerations.

Since the stages relate to the structure of moral judgment, it might be inferred that anyone who can reason logically would be rated at one of the more advanced stages; yet such ratings would be fallacious because a person could use logical reasoning effectively but still not act morally. Kohlberg claims that advanced moral reasoning depends upon logical reasoning — it is necessary for moral development and sets limits to it; however, most individuals are higher in logical stage than moral stage.

Kohlberg has recognized, in light of certain philosophical criticisms of his theory, that an adequate psychological theory that explains why a person moves from one stage to the next needs an adequate philosophical explanation as to why a higher stage is more adequate than a lower stage.[12] Such developments are different than the learning of cultural roles and systems of thought based on cultural or ethical relative views. Relativism can be classified into three types: *descriptive relativism* holds that basic ethical beliefs of different people and societies are divergent and conflicting; *normative relativism* states that what is right and good for one individual or society is not right or good for another; and *meta-ethical relativism* holds that there is no valid or rational way of justifying one set of ethical judgments against another.[13]

Kohlberg cites illustrations from psychoanalysis, anthropology, and other fields to show the problems of relativism (though Kohlberg lumps normative and meta-ethical relativism under the rubric "ethical relativism"). One example is where a patient asks his analyst why his striving for power is inauthentic and bad; he is then told that it is based on anxiety; and when the patient wants to know why that makes it bad, the psychoanalyst says that such terms can-

---

[12]Kohlberg, Lawrence: From *is* to *ought*: How to commit the naturalistic fallacy and get away with it in the study of moral development. In *The Philosophy of Moral Development: Moral Stages and the Idea of Justice*. New York, Harper & Row, 1981, pp. 101-189.
[13]Frankena, William K.: *Ethics*, 2nd ed. Englewood Cliffs, N.J., Prentice-Hall, 1973, p. 109.

not be logically analyzed—only scientific ones are subject to such analysis. Another example is anthropologists' confusion of cultural tolerance with cultural relativism by trying to show that no principles are universalizable; consequently, the values of white imperialistic nations were not better than those native people that they ruled. A third fallacy is to confuse scientific thinking in the social sciences with value neutralism. But value "neutrality" is not neutral becaue it prejudges the facts by assuming that there are no culturally universal values.

A more moderate brand of relativism, sociological relativism, holds that moral terms and judgments are used in all cultures, while the content of morality varies according to the culture. Kohlberg, in response, contends that there is less variation in cultures than is usually imagined because all cultures use basic moral categories, concepts, or principles; and all individuals, whatever the culture, go through the same sequence of moral development. But, one may ask, why does such great moral diversity exist among cultures? Kohlberg's explanation is that the differences lie in the stage of moral development of individuals and cultures and in the meaning, use, and hierarchical ordering of value concepts. These cultural divergencies are not only found in the knowledge base but in the principles used in moral evaluations. Nevertheless, the stages of moral development, Kohlberg concludes, are culturally universal, occur in an invariant developmental order, and the interpretations of the categories are universal.[13]

The claim that the higher stage's mode of judgment is more adequate than a lower stage is based on the conditions of morality rather than rationality or some other external factor. Kohlberg means that morality is a unique realm that has distinctive formal characteristics in formulating moral judgments: impersonality, universalizability, ideality, preemptiveness, and other features. In other words, moral reasons have these characteristics. Thus this is part of his theory's formalism—its emphasis on the form of moral judgment rather than the content.

---

[13]Kohlberg: From *is* to *ought.*

Kohlberg admits that he is committing one form of the naturalistic fallacy: asserting that what moral judgment ought to be should rest on an adequate conception of what it actually is. (It is considered a fallacy when ethical statements are reduced to factual statements, or when ethical statements are derived from factual statements.) What he actually claims is that it has been shown scientifically that there are universal moral forms centering on the principle of justice; science, therefore, can determine whether a philosopher's conception of morality accords with psychological facts; in turn, normative ethical analysis can show whether a particular moral philosophy can or cannot effectively handle certain moral problems that such analysis has previously delineated. Although psychological and normative analysis cannot be reduced to one another, the two are parallel or isomorphic and, consequently, the psychological descriptions of moral stages correspond to the deeper structure of normative ethics.

Assessment of the Cognitive Moral Development Theory

The cognitive moral development theory has attracted scholarly attention internationally and numerous critics and supporters have emerged. First, some criticisms of the theory are offered before drawing upon supporting evidence.

Some criticisms are directed toward the developmental stages and the logical order in the stages themselves.[14] The stages need to be delineated more precisely: the distinction between Stages 5 and 6 is not clear; conceptual links can be found between Stages 2 and 5 that do not exist between 2 and 3; and possibly more advanced stages are needed as well as finer calibration within the stages. It has also been suggested that the stages lack any necessary connection with moral action and therefore what has been provided are stages of general cognitive, rather than moral, development. Williams and Williams, on the basis of their data, believe that Stages 3 and 4 are parallel or alternate rather than sequential developmental steps.[15]

---

[14]Beck, C.M. and Others (Eds.): *Moral education: Interdisciplinary approaches*. Toronto, University of Toronto Press, 1971, pp. 355-72.
[15]Williams, N. and Williams, S.: *The Moral Development of Children*. London, Macmillan, 1970.

That individuals move through these stages in an invariant sequence is disputed by Simpson, who contends that this has only been demonstrated for Stages 2, 3, and 4.[16] Fraenkel observes a contradiction in stage formulation: if the higher stages are better, they should contain something not found in the lower stages; yet if this is the case, how will those at the lower stages understand the arguments of those at the higher stages and accept such reasoning as better than their own? But if higher is not better, there seems to be no justification for helping the young to move through the stages.[17]

Kohlberg's criticism of the "bag of virtues" approach comes under scrutiny by Peters.[18] He considers it strange to contrast a morality of principles with a morality of character traits. Being just or fair are paradigm cases of character traits; to call something a character trait — such as honesty or justness — is to suggest that someone has made a rule of his own. He adds that Kohlberg's criticism of character traits rests largely on the peculiar features of honesty as a character trait. Dishonesty has to be understood in terms of such specific situations as lying, cheating, and fraud; other virtues and vices — benevolence, cruelty, and integrity — are not ties to specific types of action. Since young children cannot grasp a principled morality (the higher stages), he recommends that they learn good habits in an intelligent way as a basis for a later period when they can determine grounds for accepting or rejecting rules. Virtues of self-control and moral courage need to be developed not only because of their value in the child's life but for their ability to sustain the individual later at the principled level so as to be able to act on principle without great stress and guilt.

Rich contends that the primary problem of Kohlberg's approach to the emotions is his assumption that emotions are irrational or nonrational forces in conflict with the cognitive core of moral development instead of his developing a cognitive approach to the emo-

[16]Simpson, Elizabeth L.: Moral development research: A case study of scientific cultural bias. *Human Development*, 17:81-106, 1974.

[17]Fraenkel, Jack, R.: The Kohlberg bandwagon: Some reservations. In Purpel, D. and Ryan, K. (Eds.): *Moral Education: It Comes with the Territory*. Berkeley, McCutchan, 1976, pp. 291-307.

[18]Peters, R.S.: Moral development: A plea for pluralism. In his *Psychology and Ethical Development*. London, Allen & Unwin, 1974, pp. 303-335. →

tions in relation to moral judgment.[19] It is claimed that to relate the cognitive developmental theory to the emotions, some use must be made of character traits. Suggestive of this reconciliation is the use of Kohlberg's treatment of motives for engaging in moral action. The character traits could therefore become patterned behavioral counterparts of the respective underlying principles in the Conventional and Postconventional levels. As examples, conscientiousness would be a primary trait at the Conventional level; compassion, benevolence, and fairness at the Postconventional level.

Gilligan notes that Kohlberg found women, in light of their strong interpersonal orientation, to favor Stage 3, a stage he held to be functional and adequate for them.[20] She laments that the traits that have conventionally defined the "goodness" of women — their care and sensitivity to the needs of others — are those that mark them as deficient in moral development. She suggests that Kohlberg's scoring system may be biased against women because of the disproportionate number of males in research samples and that the developmental theories themselves tend to be formulated by men.

Other criticisms relate to the measurement instruments employed. Kurtines and Grief question the empirical validity of the theory's basic premises because of the complexity of administering and scoring the instruments, lack of standardization in administering the tests, and the high chance of rater bias in scoring.[18] Broughton has responded to these criticisms and sought to defend the theory against these charges.[19] Carroll and Rest indicate that the scoring system has been developed over 20 years and, in contrast to Piaget's nine dimensions, it identifies hundreds of features.[20] The

---

[19]Rich, John Martin: Morality, reason and emotions. In Modgil, S. and Modgil, C. (Eds.): *Lawrence Kohlberg: Consensus and Controversy.* Sussex, England, Falmer Press, forthcoming.

[20]Gilligan, Carol: In a different voice: Women's conception of self and morality. *Harvard Educational Review,* 47:43-59, 1977.

[18]Kurtines, William and Grief, Esther B.: The development of moral thought: Review and evaluation of Kohlberg's work. *Psychological Bulletin,* 81:453-70, 1974.

[19]Broughton, John: The cognitive-developmental approach to morality. *Journal of Moral Education,* 7:81-96, January, 1978.

[20]Carroll, James L. and Rest, James R.: Moral development. In Wolman, Benjamin B. (Ed.): *Handbook of Developmental Psychology.* Englewood Cliffs, N.J.: Prentice-Hall, 1982, pp. 434-451.

system uses longitudinal as well as cross-sectional data, provides ways for handling free-response interview material, and supplies an analytical scheme for classifying the thinking of moral philosophers.

Other studies also support the theory. Do children skip stages or move through them in mixed-up order? Kuhn tested younger children at six-month intervals and found orderly progression with no evidence of skipping.[21] Kohlberg has recently completed a 20-year longitudinal study that found no skipping, with gradual change in all subjects.[22]

If the developmental stage view is correct, Turiel reports, then children should be responsible to influences that attempt to direct them to the next higher stage.[23] He employed role-playing in which children age 12 to 13 1/2 were exposed to moral reasoning at their own stage and at other stages. Children showed more of a tendency to be influenced by arguments one stage above their own than one stage below.

Rest has shown that moral judgments cannot be simply equated with verbal facility or general cognitive development, as measures of moral thinking are more closely correlated among themselves than with general cognitive ability.[24] He has also found that subjects are not 100 percent in one or another stage and, consequently, development involves gradual shifts rather than a step-by-step progression.[25]

Kohlberg has recently altered his position about moral education by claiming that such education must be partly "indoctrinative" because one cannot wait until children reach the fifth stage before dealing directly with their moral behavior.[26] The teacher, he believes, can indoctrinate or advocate without violating children's rights so long as students participate in rule-making and the value upholding process.

---

[21]Kuhn, D.: Short-term longitudinal evidence for the sequentiality of Kohlberg's early stages of moral judgment. *Developmental Psychology*, 12:162-166, 1976.

[22]Kohlberg, Lawrence: *The Meaning and Measurement of Moral Development*. Clark Lectures, Clark University, 1979.

[23]Turiel, E.: Developmental processes in the child's moral thinking. In Mussen, P.H. et al. (Eds.): *Trends and Issues in Developmental Psychology*. New York, Holt, 1969, pp. 92-133.

[24]Rest, J.R.: *Development in Judging Moral Issues*. Minneapolis: University of Minnesota Press, 1979.

[25]*Ibid.*, ch. 3.

[26]Kohlberg: Revisions in the theory and practice of moral development, pp. 84-85.

The educational applications of the theory have been to promote classroom discussion of moral issues to stimulate moral growth, and to restructure the school environment. An attempt is made in the discussion groups to arouse cognitive conflict among participants and expose them to moral reasoning of a stage higher than their own. No separate courses are proposed; rather, discussions of this type could take place in social studies, law education, philosophy and sex education.

Democratic governance, Kohlberg believes, is the basis of the "just comminity approach" whereby students learn to democratically share decision-making responsibility. One experiment along these lines is Cambridge alternative school which is run as a direct democracy. Although school rules are in effect, everyone participates in the right to interpret and enforce these rules in weekly meetings in which such decisions are made.

The first approach that raises moral issues to stimulate moral change is not a curriculum for moral education and has not been integrated into the larger curriculum. Insufficiently trained teachers in using this approach tend to misuse the stages by labelling their students. In the just community approach, students, by the second year, learned to take an active role in dealing with school problems.

In conclusion, Piaget's influence on Kohlberg's thinking was indicated, the advancements of Kohlberg's theory should be evident insofar as it has attempted to integrate (though not always successfully) philosophical, psychological, and pedagogical concerns. The theory has stimulated much research and criticism and thereby opened new ways of thinking about moral development.

LEVINSON: THE SEASONS OF ADULT LIFE CYCLES

Daniel Levinson and his associates conducted a longitudinal study of 40 men over a ten-year period using a multidisciplinary approach.[27] Recognizing that much more is known about childhood and adolescence than the adult years, the study acknowledged the

---

[27]Levinson, Daniel J., et al.: *The Seasons of a Man's Life*. New York: Knopf, 1978.

pioneer work of Jung and Erikson in the exploration of adult development while seeking to create its own framework of analysis and methodology.

The concepts developed include "life cycle," "seasons," and "era." *Life cycle* suggests that life has a certain character and follows a basic sequence. Life has a starting point and a terminating point; it has an underlying, universal pattern even though many individual and cultural variations can be observed.

Seasons signify stages or periods within the life cycle. Seasons vary qualitatively and are not simple, continuous, and unchanging. A season is a relatively stable part of the total cycle. Each season has its own internal time and no season is more important than any other one, as each contributes to the whole and is a part of the total cycle.

An *era* is a time of life that has distinctive and unifying qualities that are more inclusive than a developmental stage. The four eras are: childhood and adolescence, early adulthood, middle adulthood, and late adulthood. The study focuses on the late teens to the late forties.

The researchers decided to limit their study to men because the differences between the sexes are sufficiently great that to study 20 men and 20 women would not do justice to either group. Chosen for the study were four subgroups of 10 men between the ages of 35 and 45, selected from four occupational categories: hourly workers in industry, business executives, university biologists, and novelists. Occupations were chosen because of the assumptions that man's work is the primary basis for his life in society and for its source of fulfillment and frustration in shaping his self-concept.

The men chosen live between Boston and New York and are drawn from a diverse sample in terms of social class, racial-ethnic-religious origins, education, and marital status. Each man was seen five to ten times for a total of ten to twenty hours in two to three months, and, in most instances, follow-up interviews occurred two years after the initial interviews. "Biographical interviewing," a central methodological feature, attempted to construct a story of each man's life. In order to elicit personal experiences, the Thematic Apperception Test was used as part of interviewing and, as a biographical supplement, the researchers drew upon some biographies from famous persons in history and imaginary figures in fiction and drama.

An understanding during the era of middle adulthood may be enhanced by the concept of "individual life structure" — the underlying pattern of an individual's life at a given time. Such patterns are comprised of an individual's occupation, love relationships, marriage and family, various social relations, and relations with oneself. Life structure can be studied by examining the critical choices an individual makes and how he deals with the consequences. One or two components play a vital role in the structure, while others are peripheral. A man may put his occupation first and later start detaching himself from it and place his family in a more central position. Important components in men's lives are occupation, marriage-family, religion, ethnicity, friendships, and leisure (usually the first two are the most important ones).

The study focuses on two eras: early adulthood and middle adulthood, with each area divided into a number of seasons or periods. The stages of the former era are listed below:

Early Adulthood

Age range	Stage
17-22	Early Adult Transition
22-28	Entering Adult World
28-33	Age 30 Transition
33-40	Settling Down

The first three periods are spoken of by Levinson as "the novice phase" because entering adulthood is more complex and prolonged than commonly imagined and it therefore takes these three periods to complete the task. The two major tasks of the first period, the Early Adult Transition, are to leave the pre-adult world and take a preliminary step into the adult world. This means that the young person must separate from the family and from individuals and groups in the pre-adult world. Part of this separation and initiation into adulthood may come through experience in the armed forces or in college attendance.

One finding was that the great majority of men in the sample formed a life in early adulthood quite different from that of their parents. The significant differences lie in values and life style rather than income or social class. Many changed their religion or married a woman of another religion; some moved into a subculture that held different values from those of their parents.

It is commonly believed that a young man enters adulthood in his early twenties and, after a period of exploration, chooses a relatively stable path. In contrast, the study found that few men build their first adult structure without considerable difficulty and occassional crisis. The two tasks of the second period, Entering the Adult World, are exploration — to look at one's options and keep them open — and to create an initial adult life structure. For most men in the late twenties their life structure is unstable and fragmented: they may have had a series of jobs but no clear occupational direction.

The Age 30 Transition, the third period in early adulthood, offers an opportunity to overcome the weaknesses in the life structure formed during the previous period and to create a more satisfactory structure. For some men an age 30 crisis ensues.

The novice phase (the first three periods) has four major tasks: forming a Dream and providing it a place in the life structure; forming mentor relationships; forming an occupation; forming love relationships, marriage and family. Levinson found that the mentoring relationship is also situated in a work setting, the mentor is usually eight to fifteen years older than the protégé and the relationship lasts two or three years on the average. The mentor functions as a transitional figure and represents a mixture of parent and peer but not exclusively one. The mentor can serve one or more functions: teacher, sponsor, host and guide, or counselor. The most crucial function is that the mentor facilitate "the realization of the Dream." The "dream" is initially a vague vision, poorly articulated to reality, of what the person would like to make of his life. Thus a developmental task is that of more clearly defining his dream and finding ways to realize it. It is the mentor who defines the dream and provides needed moral support and encouragement.

The choices of occupation and marriage confront the young man with critical decisions before he has the knowledge and self-understanding to choose wisely. Yet, to delay these decisions, may incur greater costs. Whether one chooses an occupation early or remains undecided, the process of developing an occupation extends throughout the novice phase of early adulthood. No matter how long the couple has known one another prior to marriage, Levinson found they still are not fully prepared for marriage and must strive in later periods to make the marriage work.

The two tasks of the Settling Down period, the fourth period in early adulthood, are to establish one's niche in society, and to work to advance one's personal and social abilities. At the start of the period, the individual is still a junior member in the occupational world, and he depends on others' evaluation of his progress. At the end of this period, from about age 36 to 40, he attempts "to become his own man"; that is, to become a senior member in his occupation and to become less dependent upon other individuals and institutions.

According to Levinson, since no life structure can realize all possibilities—choosing one life course involves rejecting other possibilities—developmental transitions occur during adulthood to permit the emergence of other aspects of the self. From about ages 40 to 45, the Mid-life Transition involves raising difficult questions that reassess one's life. A second task of this period is to begin moving into middle adulthood by testing new choices. And a third task is to deal with polarities that cause division in one's life.

Some of the difficult questions raised during the Mid-life Transition: What have I done with my life? What are my most basic values? What are my talents and am I using or wasting them? What are my goals? The individual recognizes at this time that some of his fundamental beliefs and values are based on illusion and therefore it is necessary to confront them through an intense process, involving grief and disappointment, joy and relief, in relinquishing some of one's illusions.

Some men make major changes during this period, such as divorce, remarriage, change in occupation; others make less dramatic changes but still experience modifications in marital relations, the empty nest (offspring leave home), and changed parental relations: parents are deceased or may now become dependent upon him, if not financially then in everyday matters that they formerly handled by themselves. Erikson speaks of this stage of ego development in the middle years as Generativity vs. Stagnation.

Four polarities are faced in midlife: young/old; creation/ destruction; masculine/feminine; attachment/separateness. Although it would appear that one could not have both polar characteristics, these tendencies are not mutually exclusive but can coexist if handled properly. For instance, during this period a man thinks more about his own death and the death of others close to him, considers destructive acts that he committed against others and those committed against him; at the same time he has a desire to become more creative. Thus he can attempt to integrate these polarities during this period. With the young/old polarity, "young" may convey the archetypal symbol of growth, openness, and potential, while "old" may symbolize stability, completion, death. The task is to relinquish some of the youthful qualities and transform other qualities so they can be integrated into one's life.

Similarly, this is a time to seek a better acceptance and integration of the other polarities. A better balance is also sought between the needs of the self and the needs of society; therefore, it is a period of learning to care more about oneself before learning to care more about others. Another problem to be resolved is to modify "the dream" so that one can learn to deal with failure, flawed successes, and illusions by evaluating success and failure in more complex terms based on the quality of experience and the intrinsic value of one's work.

Entering Middle Adulthood is the period from 45 to 50. For some the change is signaled by a "crucial marker event"—a drastic change in job or occupation, marriage or a love affair, a serious illness, or other critical disturbances. Others may show no demonstrable changes. Some men have suffered such irreparable setbacks in childhood or early adulthood that they have few resources to cope with the tasks of this period; others have formed a life structure that is connected better to the world than to the self; and still other men will find this period one of the most fulfilling of the life cycle. Those men better equipped to begin developing an integrated structure for middle adulthood have made sound provisional choices during the Midlife Transition. One must explore what options in life are open to him. Thus an integrated structure may emerge early or late in this period or not at all. Those who develop this structure are less tyrannized by the ambitions, illusions, and passions of their youth. They can also be deeply attached to others and yet still maintain their own identity.

In reassessing *Seasons*, one is struck by the study's implicit normative assumptions that are insufficiently articulated, developed, and defended. The terms "satisfactory" and "satisfactoriness" are frequently used but not developed. The reader, for instance, is informed that the Age Thirty Transition provides an opportunity for creating "a more satisfactory structure," that the final test of the Midlife Transition is the "satisfactoriness" of the structure, and that some men make "satisfactory" provisional choices during the Midlife Transition.[28] Are the choices satisfactory because one is prepared to move on to the next stage? But, as noted earlier, Levinson claimed that no season is more important than any other; yet the thrust of his study would suggest that those who remain in a period beyond a set chronological age manifest arrested growth.

In this case development has a clear direction that is desirable even if the periods do not constitute strict hierarchies. But why should development proceed in this direction? Because these are emergent development characteristics? But this assumes that what is natural and in accord with nature is desirable. By the same token the waste and destruction in nature are also desirable. This line of reasoning also commits one form of the naturalistic fallacy: defining ethical terms in nonethical terms (in this case, nature).

Levinson implies that "integration" is a normative characteristic in some periods of the life cycle; however, despite the ostensible attractiveness of integration as a concept—which, incidentally, is not well developed in the study—the process of integration combines particulars so that they fuse or coalesce and thereby lose their separate identities. In some cases these separate identities should probably be maintained and in other cases integration should be brought about; however, the study does not provide defensible grounds for making such decisions.

Although the study is said to be interdisciplinary, no consideration is given to the biologist's contribution to understanding the ag-

---

[28]*Ibid.*, pp. 84, 194, 278.

ing process. The sample is limited and does not represent those from poor and socially disadvantaged backgrounds. The sample is drawn exclusively from American men and is therefore culture bound. An inadequate account of the methodology is offered, and the study is largely descriptive rather than explanatory. Little information is provided about friendships, parenting, religious beliefs, and political activities of the men in the sample.

Despite these misgivings, the study provides a clearer understanding of American men of these and similar backgrounds, offers a structured and an intelligble approach to development, is innovative in presenting and using new concepts, provides many pertinent insights, and is written with a literary flair.

FOWLER: FAITH AND HUMAN DEVELOPMENT

James Fowler has provided a theory of faith development by describing developmental stages which individuals move through in creating conceptions of ultimate reality and answering such questions as, What is the meaning of life?[29] In developing his theory, Fowler draws upon the works of Piaget, Kohlberg, and Erikson.

"Faith," however, is not given a conventional, but a stipulative, definition in the study — and this makes a great deal of difference for the entire project. Here are some conventional definitions of faith: "firm belief in something for which there is no proof"[30] or "an attitude of belief which goes beyond the available evidence."[31] It is necessary, then, to examine the stipulative definition to ascertain whether Fowler is warranted in employing it in terms of success or failure in generating fruitful and creative ideas.

Faith helps to shield us from our nakedness and provide the courage to face the abyss that surrounds us. It helps us to develop an ultimate environment, a dependable life span. Faith is universal,

---

[29]James W. Fowler: *Stages of Faith: The Psychology of Human Development and the Quest for Meaning.* San Francisco, Harper & Row, 1981.

[30]*Webster's Ninth New Collegiate Dictionary.* Springfield, Mass., Merrian-Webster, 1983.

[31]Reese, W.L.: *Dictionary of Philosophy and Religion: Eastern and Western Thought.* Atlantic Highlands, N.J., Humanities Press, 1980, p. 166.

whether one is a Hindu, Christian, or Marxist. Each person is born with a capacity for faith, but it requires a nurturing environment to grow. Faith is not always religious, as it can apply to nontheists as well. It is the way that individuals find coherence and meaning in their lives; it is a person's way of relating to others against a backdrop of shared meaning and purpose.

What is this quality of life? It is an active mode: a way of trusting, committing, and relating to the world; and by these commitments, as in the family (but not limited to the family), values are conferred that may be of transcendent worth. Thus, linkages are formed with others and institutions which we play a part; these linkages are based on trust and loyalty.

Drawing upon the writings of theologian H. Richard Niebuhr, Fowler identifies three major types of faith-identity relations: polytheistic, henotheistic, and radical monotheistic. A pattern of faith and identity that lacks an organizing center of interest is *polytheistic*. Such persons can never bring all of their concerns to any value commitment or relationship. This type is expressed in the consumer society desire to own anything one wants and have intimate relations with whomever one wishes.

In contrast, the *henotheistic* type invests deeply in a center of value and power, but finds it to be false, inappropriate, and not something of ultimate concern. One invests in projects of self-justification, such as quests for wealth, success, and fame, to bolster the sense of self. In its extreme form, it becomes a fetish in its focus on a narrow and exclusive value center that takes such forms as careerism and workaholism, or where sex and money become gods.

The *radical monotheistic* type finds people relating to one another through bonds of trust and loyalty in which they relinquish their tribal gods and identify with a universal community. It is a regulative point of view that prevents our limited faiths from becoming idolatrous.

Thus faith itself, according to Fowler, is a way of seeing our life in terms of holistic images; our knowledge begins with images and is stored in images. An *image* is a vague inner representation and one's feeling about a state of affairs. Images, therefore, precede concepts and are deeper than them. In answering a question put to us, the first stage of shaping a response is to scan images to discover what we know about something. The world's religions, for instance, evoke the imagery of the ultimate conditions of existence. But because some person's imagery of an "ultimate environment" (the ultimate conditions of existence) may be impersonal, indifferent, or randomly chaotic rather than structured and coherent does not mean that it is not an image of faith. The opposite of faith is nihilism, not doubt. It is the nihilist who despairs in finding any meaning in life and is unable to image a transcendent environment.

Fowler acknowledges his indebtedness to Erikson, Piaget, and Kohlberg; he also indicates that Daniel Levinson's concept of eras enters into his thinking about stages. To acquaint the reader with the first three theorists, he provides a fictional conversation among them about each stage in the life cycle. Erikson's works have formed a backdrop for Fowler's thinking; whereas since Fowler's stage theory is a form of structuralism, he has been influenced more directly by Piaget and Kohlberg. But in contrast to the latter two figures, Fowler has tried to incorporate knowing, valuing, and imaging in each stage. He envisions the stages as generalizable descriptions of integrated sets of knowing and valuing that are invariant. Each stage carries forward and integrates operations of all previous stages. No claim is made that the stages are universal, as they have yet to be tested cross-culturally. The faith stages, however, are neither achievement levels by means of which the worth of persons is evaluated, nor are they therapeutic or educational goals. The educational task is to seek the full values of faith at each stage and help to rework faith when undergoing a transition to the next stage.

From 1972 to 1981 Fowler and his associates conducted 359 taped, in-depth faith development interviews. Each interview lasted two to two and one-half hours and comprised a life review (biography), life-shaping experiences and relationships, present values and commitments, and religious beliefs. Most of the interviews were conducted in Boston and Toronto with persons of differing ages (ranging from 3.5 to 84), sex, race, and religion.

Faith Stages

Undifferentiated Faith (Infancy)
1. Intuitive-Projective Faith (Early Childhood)
2. Mythic-Literal Faith (School Years)
3. Synthetic-Conventional Faith (Adolescence)
4. Individuative-Reflective Faith (Young Adulthood)
5. Conjunctive Faith (Mid-life and Beyond)
6. Universalizing Faith

Undifferentiated faith is a pre-stage in which the seeds of positive emotions (love, trust) are being formed and contend with various fears about the infant's environment (abandonment, deprivation, and the like). The transition to the first stage emerges with the acquisition of language.

Stage 1 is a fantasy-filled imitative phase in which the child can be permanently influenced by the faith propagated. Thought patterns are fluid and imagination is uninhibited by rational thought. Knowing is dominated by perception, and the imagination creates both positive and negative feelings that thought in later years will have to sort out. The first awareness of sex and death arises at this stage.

Beginning in Stage 2, the child begins to acquire the beliefs, stories, and observances symbolic of one's community. Beliefs and moral rules are interpreted literally. The emergence of concrete operations limits and organizes the previous stage's dominance by imagination. The child learns how to take the perspective of others and to reciprocate. The child can be deeply affected by dramatic tales that tend to be anthropomorphized. Stories and myths are ways of giving coherence to experience, but the stories are not subject to reflection at this stage.

A person's experience extends outside the family in Stage 3. Because of involvement with school or work, peers, the media, and perhaps religion, faith's role is to synthesize values and information from divergent sources to form a sense of identity and a perspective on life. Although this stage arises in adolescence, it becomes a permanent stopping point for many adults. Persons are sensitively attuned to the expectation and judgment of others and are unable to develop autonomous judgment or an independent perspective; the expectations of others become strongly internalized, making it difficult to move to the next stage. The actual transition to the next stage may be precipitated by contradictions between valued sources of authority or experiences that lead to serious reflection about one's beliefs and values.

Although Stage 4 may emerge in young adulthood, for some adults it does not arise until the mid-thirties or forties, and, as noted above, some adults never leave Stage 3. The self in Stage 4 is no longer composed of the viewpoints of other persons and one's roles, but one's self-identity is differentiated from others. The person translates symbols into conceptual meanings and seeks to banish myths; it is a stage for critical reflection about one's identity and ideology. A transition to the next stage may occur when the individual, having been inattentive to the unconscious level, experiences anarchic and disturbing inner voices that conjure childish past images. A recognition that life is more complex than the logic that this stage envisions presses one to a more dialectical and multileveled approach to life.

The self-certainty of Stage 4 gives way to the integration of unrecognized and suppressed elements that shape Stage 5. Here the individual becomes open to the deeper self and begins to reclaim and reshape one's past. The dialectical feature is alive to paradox and seeks to unify opposition. One can perceive one's own or one's group's most significant meanings while recognizing their relativity and distortion. Danger, however, lies in one's life degenerating into complacency or cynical withdrawal in the face of paradoxical truth. Only a few are able to make the radical actualization called for in the next stage.

Stage 6 overcomes the paradox by a moral and ascetic actualization. No longer heeding the dangers to oneself or to one's primary groups, the individual acts on imperatives of absolute love and justice. These few individuals at Stage 6 may undergo nonviolent suffering to show respect for all human beings. They hold open fellowship with persons at any other stages and faiths. They seek to transform the world in accordance with a divine and transcendent image. These persons are not perfect, nor are they identical to

Maslow's "self-actualized person" or Roger's "fully functioning human being." Representatives of Stage 6 are Gandhi, Martin Luther King, Jr. (in the last years of his life), and Mother Teresa of Calcutta. Also included are Dag Hammarskjold, Dietrich Bonhoeffer, Abraham Heschel, and Thomas Merton (this stage is similar to Kohlberg's Stage Seven).

In augmenting our understanding of this stage theory, Fowler envisions the stages as dynamically connected in a spiral, with each successive stage linked to and adding to the previous ones. Certain life issues that confront faith recur at each stage; yet each stage approaches these issues at a new level of complexity. Transitions from one stage are frequently painful, protracted, and unsuccessful. Although there are minimum chronological ages below which a stage is not likely to begin, the transitions are not inevitable or automatic. The *contents* of the individual's faith (as opposed to its structure) consist of centers of value (those concerns of greatest worth), images of power (that which sustains the individual in difficult times), and master stories (our interpretive stories about events that affect our lives). By applying this formulation, Fowler is able to explain *conversion* as a change in the contents of faith. It involves recentering our centers of value and images of power and consciously adopting a new set of master stories for reshaping our lives.

A serious problem in some communities is that educational, religious, and governance practices promote a lower stage for adults. In these communities the modal level is in terms of Synthetic-Conventional Faith (Stage 3) or just beyond it. One way Fowler suggests for moving beyond this level is not to shrink from conflict, doubt and struggle. A faith community needs to call forth the strength of each stage of faith.

In assessing Fowler's theory of faith, some problems should be noted. His sample is not random; it is overrepresented by some groups (Jews) and underrepresented by others (Blacks). He admits that no research has been conducted with Eastern religions and traditions. It should be evident, however, that in places he leans heavily on the Judaeo-Christian heritage: in Stage 6 love (New Testament) and justice (Old Testament) are the overriding values. Since Stage 5 and 6 are undergirded by substantive moral and religious views while the stages themselves are considered invariant, one might seriously question the universality of the stage theory (though he does not claim universality). Yet the hierarchical nature implies that later stages are superior to earlier ones. Just as with Kohlberg's theory, one needs an explanation as to how someone can grasp a higher stage in order to make the transition from a lower stage. If one could conceptually grasp the next stage, then the individual would be partly at the higher stage. Perhaps Fowler's ideas about what causes transitions will be of help here.

Some theologians may challenge his distinction between faith, religion, and belief; and his stipulative definition of faith, if rejected, would undermine his study. Others may question whether the dynamics of faith can actually be linked to human development.

Despite these misgivings, Fowler has created the most powerful developmental theory of faith in the literature by organizing his own investigations in light of what he has learned from Erikson, Piaget, and Kohlberg. He has sought to overcome the limitations of the latter two figures' structuralism by creating a place for content and providing in each stage cognitive, affective, and image dimensions. And he has shown how faith can be nurtured and can continue to grow over a lifetime.

LOEVINGER: MILESTONES OF EGO DEVELOPMENT

Mirroring the blind spots of history in general, the focal point for the history of moral development theory has been the study of men. Freud viewed women through stained glass, referring to them as "a dark continent for psychology."[32] Piaget tested his cognitive development theory by utilizing the game of marbles and story-telling techniques with young boys. Kohlberg omitted women from the original sample which became the basis for his longitudinal survey of developmental modes of moral reasoning.[33]

---

[32]Freud, Sigmund: The question of lay analysis. In *The Standard Edition of the Complete Psychological Works of Sigmund Freud*, (Vol. 20), p. 212.
[33]Kohlberg, Lawrence: The development of modes of moral thinking and choice in the years ten to sixteen. Unpublished doctoral dissertation. University of Chicago, 1958.

In recent years, certain investigators, primarily female scholars, have attempted to recast moral development by unearthing hidden dimensions of feminine experience. These emergent paradigms are perhaps best represented in Jane Loevinger's model of ego development and in Carol Gilligan's work in psychological theory and women's development. Loevinger and Gilligan seek to reframe Kohlbergean theory; however, their resepctive positions assume different purposes and therefore create different visions for future constructions of moral development. Whereas Loevinger implies that the broad contours of her theory might apply to males as well as females, Gilligan intimates that her study attempts to redefine moral experience via uniquely feminine perspectives.

Loevinger's inquiry is undergirded by a wide range of prior influences, including the following: psychoanalytic theory; Harry Stack Sullivan's revisions of ego psychology, particularly his notions on interpersonal analysis; theories of character development by Peck and Havighurst; Maslow's formulation of the "self-actualized" person; stage theories of cognitive moral development (Piaget and Kohlberg); and Adler's concept of "style of life," i.e., one's "method of facing problems, opinion about oneself and the problems of life, and the whole attitude toward life."[34]

Given these complementary foundational sources, Loevinger poses the "search for coherent meanings in experience" to focus her own theoretical inquiry. H.S. Sullivan's theory of ego stability, or *anxiety-gating*, is at the base of Loevinger's general speculations. Sullivan uses the term "anxiety-gating" to show how a person, by *selective inattention*, normally focuses upon patterns of experience which coincide with his/her existing self-system, or ego. Thus the aim of ego

[34]Loevinger, Jane and Wessler, Ruth: *Measuring Ego Development*, (Vol. I). San Francisco, Jossey-Bass, 1970, p. 7. Also see Sullivan, Harry Stack: *The Interpersonal Theory of Psychiatry*. New York, Norton, 1953; Peck Robert F. and Havighurst, Robert J.: *The Psychology of Character Development*. New York, Wiley, 1960; Maslow, Abraham H.: *Motivation and Personality*. New York, Harper, 1954; Piaget, Jean: *The Moral Judgment of the Child*. London, Kegan Paul, 1932; Kohlberg, Lawrence: Development of moral character and moral ideology. In M. Hoffman and L.W. Hoffman (Eds.), *Review of Child Development Research*, (Vol. I). New York, Sage Foundation, 1964, pp. 383-431; and Adler, Alfred: *The Individual Psychology of Alfred Adler*, H.L. Ansbacher and R.R. Ansbacher (Eds.). New York, Basic Books, 1956, p. 174.

maintenance and growth becomes the selective gating out of experiential observations at odds with present ego functions.[35]

These theoretical constructs are made more concrete in Loevinger's studies of women by way of the assessment of "sentence completion" testing. In this evaluation, subjects are given "word stems" (e.g., "I feel sorry . . ." or "When they avoided me . . .") and are then asked to complete each stem in their own words and thoughts (e.g., one might respond to the preceding stems, " . . . for my mistakes" or " . . . I felt hurt and alone"). Notice should be taken that Loevinger's method is a form of psychoanalytic *projective* testing, a relatively unstructured technique which aims at revealing subjects' *affective* as well as cognitive thought patterns. While Kohlberg's methodology is focused at the cognitive level, and mainly attuned to variables in judgmental *reasoning*, Loevinger seeks to tap wider, more subtle, sources of referential response in the person's variegated attitudes and experience. Thus, as with Gilligan's studies, Loevinger's content and process material highlights *emotional dilemmas and conflicts* about morality in ways which escape attention in Kohlberg's discussion.

Loevinger applies the qualitative findings of projective testing to the quantitative measures of psychometrics. On the basis of these findings, she has formulated an eight-stage theory of ego development, sometimes referred to as "milestones of development," as follows (Kohlberg's analogous stages are listed in parentheses):

1. Presocial
2. Symbiotic
3. Impulsive (orientation to Punishment and Obedience)
4. Self-protective (Naively Hedonistic orientation)
5. Conformist ("Good Boy" orientation)
6. Conscientious (orientation to Authority, Law and Order)
7. Autonomous (Contractual orientation)
8. Integrated (Principled orientation)[36]

---

[35]Loevinger, Jane and Wessler, Ruth: *Measuring Ego Development*, (Vol. I), pp. 7-8.

[36]*Ibid.*, pp. 10-11. Subsequent sentence-completion illustrations are excerpted from this work. For a succinct view of Loevinger's model in relation to other theories, see Breger, Louis: *From Instinct to Identity: The Development of Personality.* Englewood Cliffs, Prentice-Hall, 1974, pp. 283-294. Breger's analysis is especially instructive in comparing Loevinger with Kohlberg.

Loevinger places each stage in the context of distinctive dilemmas or conflicts which individuals appear to undergo in an effort to ensure "impulse control" in their "character" development. These parameters bespeak Loevinger's own reliance on "ego strength" and other constructs in ego psychology; moreover, they indicate that she may be mixing "character" development with "moral" development.

Stages 1 and 2 are characterized by the crude emergence of the ego, or self, in a rather undifferentiated state. Here the infant and young child must learn to adapt, to link their *presocial* selves to immediate, but wider, social relationships. Such bonds are first joined in *symbiotic* relations with parent figures. As a result of these ties, the child will normally become "impulsive," e.g., negativistic and self-assertive. At the *impulse* stage (Stage 3), individual thought and action is usually governed by anticipation of reward or punishment. For example, in the child's mind, "good guys give to me, mean ones don't." Loevinger's studies present some case material from adult sentence completion responses which illustrates how individuals carry the baggage of impulsivity into later life:

A woman should always — *keep clean.*
Usually she felt that sex — *is good to me because I get hot.*

Stage 4, or the *self-protective* stage, is arrived at when the person begins to transcend narrow impulsive behavior, thereby incorporating concepts of "right" and "wrong," or blameworthiness, into her character structure. However, feelings of self-control and self-mastery over situations, circumstances, and other persons are still not adequately resolved at this stage. Indeed, there may well be so-called "malignant" signs at this stage, e.g., opportunism, deception, coercion, and manipulation and exploitation of others. Such behavioral signposts correspond to H.S. Sullivan's notion of "malevolent transformation." As examples of "self-protective" ideation, Loevinger cites the following sentence completion responses:

A woman should always — *be alert and on guard.*
A woman's body — *is made for the enjoyment of men.*
My mother and I — *get along when she has money.*

The *conformist* stage (Stage 5) reflects Loevinger's findings, roughly in tandem with Kohlberg's broad "conventional-stage" morality, that most people tend to mirror the attitudes, beliefs, and values of those around them. Thus external measures, rather than inner conflictual response, remain at the forefront in this stage. The following sentence completion responses are indicative of the "conformist" period in one's life (which Kohlberg and Loevinger insist most of us never outgrow):

> When I am with a man — *I try to act like a lady.*
> Being with other people — *is the best thing to do.*

Not until Stage 6, the level of *conscientiousness*, does the individual markedly move in the direction of self-decision and personal goal attainment. Loevinger traces this stage to late-adolescent or young-adult kinds of moral thinking and action and claims that it is especially noticeable in college students. It is also a decidedly confusing, tormenting period inasmuch as the young person must weigh past, safer, routes of conventional wisdom with new inroads made by increasing psychological and experiential awareness. That tension is reflected in these sentence completion responses:

> A good mother — *is hard to define.*
> A wife should — *try to understand and sympathize.*
> My conscience bothers me if — *I don't do what I believe is fair or right.*

At the *autonomous* stage (Stage 7), the maturing individual undergoes deepened inner conflct; more sophisticated sensitivity to concrete situations, processes, and change; increasing respect for others' rights and interpersonal relations; and a quickening search for reflective self-fulfillment. Such strivings are articulated in these sentence completion responses:

> My mother and I — *are independent though devoted.*
> When people are helpless — *it is best to aid them to help themselves than to prolong their helplessness and dependency on others.*
> I am — *striving to experience as many things as I can and get a broad view of how the human race lives.*

Finally, an exceedingly small number of people (Loevinger estimates not more than one percent of any given group) enter Stage 8, in which *integrated* reconciliation of previous conflicts and polarizations takes place. These persons are able to deal with paradox and ambiguity, to value justice and idealism, to oppose all manner of prejudice, to manage inner conflict, to appreciate mutuality in relationships, and to do all this with a modicum of existential humor and wisdom. In the unlikely event one should happen to meet such individuals, these vivid examples from Loevinger's sentence completion responses might be helpful for the purpose of identification:

> The worst thing about being a woman — *cannot be generalized, as one woman makes an asset of the same situation decried by another.*
> A good mother — *lets go, loves without demanding conformity to her own ideals and standards — and helps to guide if possible.*

Though Loevinger acknowledges that there are doubtless "well-adjusted" people at all her stages and that her scale should not be taken as a "moral IQ" index, she also admits that we live in a "conformist's world" where some feel happy and others fall into various forms of mental illness. Accordingly, Loevinger suggests that *coping mechanisms*, rather than problem solving, may offer the most fruitful tools for moral and psychological well-being in the long run.

Even though her theory makes use of a rich variety of sources (a circumstance which might be at the root of some of her methodological problems), Loevinger grants that there are numerous difficulties in her investigation. First, there may in fact be no necessary correspondence between "a given bit of behavior" as exemplified in the sentence-completion exercises and those attitudes which might underlie any such given responses. That is, Loevinger casts her theory at a "probabilistic" level. Second, there are doubtless myriad kinds of development proceeding along with ego development, thus making for fuzzy boundaries of distinction among such areas as "cognitive," "psychosexual," and "moral" development. (Indeed, the term "ego" itself represents a very tenuous borderland for conceptual analysis.) Next, there are companion difficulties in ascertaining distinct levels of development since most behavior is typically manifested at more than one level. Moreover, Loevinger recognizes the related problem of assigning behavioral and attitudinal signs to any particular developmental level. Finally, she is admirably honest in acknowledging perhaps the weakest link in her entire theory:

> No behavioral task can be guaranteed to display just what one wants to know about ego level. Neither a structured test nor an unstructured test

carries a guarantee . . . . There is always a chance that a person can conceal all . . .[37]

Indeed, we all may sometimes hide our underlying motives and the reasons for our ordinary behavior in the everyday life of moral action.

GILLIGAN: IN A DIFFERENT VOICE

A colleague of Kohlberg in Harvard's Center for Moral Education, Carol Gilligan has challenged his theories in light of her own research on women. While Gilligan's model of women's moral development is not in finished form, still needs to be further tested, and is couched in highly speculative, intuitive language, it nonetheless counterposes a rich tapestry of *particular social and personal context* alongside Kohlberg's more abstractly contemplative universe of discourse. The basic thrust of Gilligan's thesis underscores a language of care, responsibility, and not wanting to hurt others in women's presumably unique moral thema and moral vision.

According to Gilligan, women speak "in a different voice" than men. Extrapolating on Kohlberg's studies, Gilligan hypothesizes that women's language is substantially one of caring and interpersonal responsibility whereas men's dialect seems to be framed in terms of individual rights, liberties, duties, and their attendant protection. Some critics have argued that the rather warm reception of Kohlberg's paradigm may be explained in part by its tendency to "reinforce current dominant views about pluralistic democracy and justice as fairness."[38] In other words, Kohlberg's model of justice may be part and parcel of that strong core of "liberal individualism" so popular in Western culture.[39]

How does Gilligan conceptualize the development of "self" and "other"? She takes an evolutionary stance attuned to the subjective

---

[37]Loevinger, Jane and Wessler, Ruth: *Measuring Ego Development*, (Vol. I), p. 9.

[38]Sichel, Betty A.: Moral development and eduation: men's language of rights and women's language of responsibility. *Contemporary Education Review*, 2:34, Spring, 1983.

[39]See Pateman, Carole: The "disorder of women": women love, and the sense of justice. *Ethics*, 91:20-34, 1980, for a similar assessment of Rousseau, Freud, and other major figures in Western thought.

passages of those women whom she interviews in her studies. (To her credit, Gilligan's action research is carried on with women who *actually* face extraordinary personal moral dilemmas, e.g., whether to have an abortion. Her technique seems more realistic than the imaginary, hypothetical questions posed in Kohlberg's experiments.) The fluid growth sequence in women's ethic of care appears to follow: (1) "an initial focus on caring for the self in order to ensure survival"; (2) "a transitional phase in which this judgment is criticized as selfish"; and (3) "a new understanding of the connection between self and others which is articulated by the concept of responsibility."[40]

Gilligan further contends that this "new understanding" of relatedness would be vitiated if one were to gauge women's moral development solely with reference to Kohlberg's theoretical interpretations. In her interviews with 11-year-old children, Amy and Jake, Gilligan attempts to show how Amy's evident moral virtues would be minimized if she were judged by Kohlberg's categories. Using Kohlberg's classic Heinz case (stealing from the druggist to save the life of one's spouse), Gilligan's interviews reveal different responses from Amy and Jake. The latter solves the Heinz issue in a manner akin to the algebraic gymnastic he performs in mathematics class: who has the property right and what is fair for the individual? Amy, on the other hand, is more intent on making sure that Heinz and his wife do not suffer in their relationship as a result of any theft. On Kohlberg's scale of values, Amy's compassionate logic would be insufficiently informed by principles of moral *reasoning*, which presumably emphasize fairness, justice, and rights.

Yet Gilligan's own interpretations would have to bear much the same critical scrutiny that has been applied to Kohlberg's studies, especially in terms of their predictive power. Gilligan also admits that her samples are "small and nonrepresentative," including mostly upper-middle-class children and Radcliffe-Harvard students.[41] Of the three studies referred to in her largest work, *In a Different Voice*, the total sample size is 144 (8 males and 8 females at varying ages at

[40]Gilligan, Carol: *In a Different Voice: Psychological Theory and Women's Development*. Cambridge: Harvard U.P., 1982, p. 74.

[41]Murphy, J.M. and Gilligan, Carol: Moral development in late adolescence and adulthood: a critique and reconstruction of Kohlberg's theory. *Human Development*, 23:84, 1980.

nine points across the life cycle, i.e., ages 6-9, 11, 15, 19, 22, 25-27, 35, 45, and 60); this sample includes a "more intensively interviewed subsample of 36 (2 males and 2 females at each age)."[42]

Other critics have raised more substantive questions concerning Gilligan's distinctions on assumed male versus female ethical differences. As one writer has observed, ". . . the ethical differences that emerge in interviews with males and females documented by Gilligan might better be summarized as variations in expressions of care and responsibility.[43] Kohlberg himself addresses the issue by claiming that once women take on the same social roles as men, women's moral development will likely be the same as that of men. (Of course, as the preceding discussion makes evident, no one has really proven that women's moral development is any less, more, or different than that of men.)

It may well be a behavioral truism that most people act in similar ways when placed in similar situations under similar conditions. However, since full conditions of sexual social equality have not yet been legitimized, one might do well to recall that such libertarians as John Stuart Mill (for his time, a sympathizer in women's causes) and John C. Calhoun (an unabashed advocate of slavery) each appealed to the achievement of certain levels of autonomous moral development before they would assent to substantial rights for minority groups. This warning seems tangential to Kohlberg's argument about equivalent social roles, but it nonetheless bespeaks crucial, sometimes hidden, elements in the underside of the history of ideas.

Nor do Gilligan's sensitive explorations of androgyny and moral boundaries directly address wider social and political concerns. Like Lawrence Blum, she postulates social relationships which are largely restricted to personal relations among family members, friends, and colleagues. Gilligan's "new maps" do not precisely touch on "the possibility of aspiring beyond liberal goals of distributive justice and the satisfaction of private interest" which might form social bonds dedicated to "the ideals of affective, productive, and rational community."[44]

---

[42]Gilligan, Carol: *In A Different Voice*, p. 3.

[43]Prakash, Madhu Suri: Review of *In a Different Voice: Psychological Theory and Women's Development*. In *Educational Studies*, 15:194, Summer, 1984.

[44]Wolff, Robert Paul: *The Poverty of Liberalism*. Boston, Beacon, 1968, pp. 183-184. Also see Rawls, John: *A Theory of Justice*. Cambridge, Harvard U.P., 1971.

In this shortcoming, Gilligan joins forces with Blum, who has also articulated a "two-strained" portrait of morality: one of Kantian rights and impartiality, the other of primary human feeling— "sympathy, compassion, and human concern."[45] This historical development in moral development theory has roots at least as old as Alfred Adler (and the ancient Greek Stoics whom he so admired). Adler believed that the emotions and reason fuel each other and that any artificial dichotomy separating them begged obvious issues in the way humans interact. Gilligan and Blum are also interested in a morality of interaction, but one "that is prerequisite to the fulfillment of . . . individual goals."[46] Instead Adler spoke in terms of changing social conditions which obstructed social equality and moral community. Recent empirical evidence tends to confirm that engagement in actual social interaction, particularly interactions of relative equality, may in fact be the most effective way to develop a morality of tolerance for a truly moral community.[47] Adler pointed the way to such a moral pattern for *both* men and women.[48]

[45]Blum, Lawrence A.: *Friendship, Altruism and Morality*. London, Routledge and Kegan Paul, 1980, p. 8.

[46]*Ibid.*, p. 98.

[47]See Serow, Robert C.: *Schooling for Social Diversity: An Analysis of Policy and Practice*. New York, Teachers College Press, 1983, especially chapters 2 and 3.

[48]DeVitis, Joseph L.: Freud, Adler, and women: Powers of the "weak" and "strong." *Educational Theory*, in press. For a recent empirical analysis which challenges Gilligan's findings, see Walker, Lawrence J.: Sex differences in the development of moral reasoning: a critical review. *Child Development* 55: 677-691, 1984.

INDEX

A

Abandonment, 108
Absolutistic thought, 48-49
Academic atmosphere, 79
Academic dishonesty, 67
Acceptance, 71, 103
Accessibility, faculty, 71
Accommodation, 71
Accountability, moral, 3, 16
Achievement, 60, 77, 107
Action, moral, 94-96
Activism, political, 84
Activators, inner-life, 78-79
Acts
 dishonest, 89-90
 honest, 89-90
Adaptation, 61-62, 81-83, 90-91
Adler, Alfred, 4, 14, 22-33, 41, 49, 52, 64,
 112, 120 (*see also* Individual Psychology)
Adler, Gerhard, 34, 40-41
Adolescence, 4, 7, 34, 48-49, 53-55, 58-
 63, 74, 98-99, 108
Adolescent ideology, 63
Advising, 79-80
Advocacy, 79-80
Adulthood, 7, 9, 27, 44-45, 48, 53-55, 60-
 62, 83-85, 89, 98-103, 108-109
Adventure, 84
Aesthetics, 73, 78, 84
Affective competencies, 61
Affective thought, 111-120
Affluent youth, 85
Age 30 Transition, 100-101, 104
Agentic development, 32

Aggression, 19, 24, 28, 33, 45-46, 77
Aging process, 104-105
Agnosticism, 84
Alienation, 5, 83-86
Allocentrism, 81-82
Altruism, 33, 54
Alumni, 83
Ambiguity, 78, 115-116
Ambition, 81
Ambivalence, 85
America (United States), 20, 81, 84
American college students, 66-86
American culture, 45-46, 50, 62, 84, 105
Amoral conduct, 6
Amoral position, 63
Anaclitic identification, 44-45
Anal stage, 60
Analysis
 interpersonal, 112
 logical, 92-93
 normative, 94
 psychological, 94
 scientific, 92-93
Analytic psychology (*see* Jung, C.G.)
Androgyny, 119
Angyal, Andras, 9-10
Anima, 40
Animus, 40
Anomie, 9, 13
Ansbacher, Heinz L., 25, 28
Ansbacher, Rowena R., 25, 28
Anthropology, 33-34, 59, 92-93
Anthropomorphism, 108
Anti-authoritarian position, 63
Anti-models, 91

121

Antimoral position, 63
Anti-Semitism, 41
Anxiety, 78, 84
Anxiety-gating, 112-113
Appeal to social conventions, 90
Aproval, 88
Archaeology, 33
Archetypes, 20, 34-35, 40, 103
Aristotle, 89
Armed forces, 100
Art, 19, 23
Artifacts, 33
Ascetic actualization, 109-110
Ascetism, 109-110
Assertiveness, 78-80
Assessment, of cognitive moral development theory, 94-98
Assessment, of developmental tasks, 56-58
Athletic physiques, 78-80
Attachment-separateness polarity, 103
Attention, focal, 47-48, 51
Attitude-behavior dichotomy, 16
Attitudes, 113-116
Attractive incentives, 42
Austria, 17, 29
Authoritarian child-rearing, 27-28
Authority, 20, 48, 61, 73-74, 88, 109, 113
Authority, obedience to, 20, 75
Authority, omniscient, 74-75
Authority, orientation, 88, 113
Autocentrism, 81-82
Autonomous level of moral development, 88-89
Autonomous morality, 48-49
Autonomous stage, 113-115
Autonomous striving, 10
Autonomy, 4, 8-13, 33, 48-50, 60, 69, 82-83, 108-109, 119
Avocational interests, 70
Awareness, 115

B

Bag of virtues, 89, 95
Bakan, David, 32
Baltes, P., 91
Bandura, Albert, 42-44
Basic repression, 28-29
Beatniks, 61, 84
Beck, C.M., 94

Becoming autonomous, 69, 72
Behavior
  acquisition, 7
  bad, 42-43
  deviant, 9
  evaluation, 72-73
  good, 42-43
  group, 54
  learned, 7
  moral, 97-98
  right, 88
  socially responsible, 54
  specific, 89-90
  species-specific, 7
Behavioral child rearing, 28, 42-46
Behavioral engineering, 38
Behavioral models, 42-43
Behavioral patterns, 96
Behavioral science methodologies, 6-7
Behavioral signs, 116
Behaviorism, 44
Belief(s), 70, 102, 105-111, 115
Benevolence, 72, 95-96
Berkely Free Speech movement, 85-86
Bettelheim, Bruno, 52
Bias, scoring, 96
Bigotry, 57-58
Biological viewpoint, 24
Biologists, 99, 104-105
Biographical interviewing, 99-100
Biography, 55, 99-100, 107
Bisexual diffusion, 60
Black Muslims, 61
Black people, 110
Black Power, 61
Black protest, 85
Blameworthiness, 114
Blaming the victim, 23
Blank slate, 33
Blum, Lawrence A., 31, 119-120
Bodily stimulation, 55
Body types, 80
Bonhoefer, Dietrich, 110
Boston, 99, 107
Boy Scout bag, 89
Breger, Louis, 113
Britain, 90
Bronfenbrenner, Urie, 50
Broughton, John, 96

Buddha, 14
Business executives, 99

C

Calcutta, 110
Calhoun, John C., 119
Cambridge alternative school, 98
Canada, 90
Capitalism, 81
Care, 31, 96, 103, 117-119
Career choice, 61, 75
Careerism, 106
Caretaker figure, 45
Carroll, James L., 96
Castration anxiety, 20-21, 28
Categorical imperative, 73, 89 (*see also* Kant, Immanuel)
Categories, moral, 93
Center for Moral Eduation, 117 (*see also* Harvard University)
Center, organizing, 106
Center, value, 110
Ceremonies, 54-55, 62
Certainty, 109
Change
  institutional, 65
  situational, 115
  social, 12, 65, 85
  socio-educational, 23
Character
  development, 11, 56-58, 112-114
  traits, 7, 89-90, 95-96
Character Education Inquiry, 89-90
Charismatic figures, 14
Cheating, 48, 95
Checklist of Educational Views (CLEV), 74
Chicago, 90
Chickering, Arthur W., v, 5, 66-73
Child abuse and neglect, 26
Child guidance clinics, 29
Childhood, 4, 7, 17-18, 26, 33-36, 42-45, 48-54, 75, 85, 89-91, 95-99, 103, 108, 114
Child rearing, 17, 40-46
Children's rights, 97
Christ, 14
Christian ethics, 73
Christianity, 63, 105-106, 110

Christian Middle Ages, 81
Church, 7
Church-related colleges, 73
Circle figure, 33, 38
Citizenship, 54-55, 67, 81
Civic competence, 54, 56
Civilization, 19, 22, 29, 52
Civil rights movement, 3, 85-86
Clarifying purpose, 70
Class, social, 54-55, 57, 99-101
Classroom
  discussion, 97-98
  rules, 45
Clinical interview technique, 47-52 (*see also* Piaget, Jean)
Codes, of conduct, 38-39
Coercion, 114
Cognitive moral development, 46-52, 58, 87-98, 11-113, 116
Cognitive-structuralism, 15-16, 46-52, 87-98
Collective education, 37
Collectivism, 32-34
College, 66-86, 100, 115
College, church-related, 73
College, faculty, 73
College orientation, 80
College students, 66-86
Concrete operations, 108
Conduct, 6, 11, 72
Cohen, Albert K., 9
Coherence, 106, 112
Commitment, 74-76, 106-107
Communication skills, 49
Community, 25, 32, 81, 106, 108, 110, 119-120
Compassion, 31, 96, 118
Competence, 69-72 (*see also* Chickering, Arthur W.)
Competition, 29, 45-46, 77
Complexity, 75-76
Comprehensiveness, logical, 88-89
Concepts
  moral, 93
  value, 93
Conceptual meaning, 109
Concern, ultimate, 106
Conflict
  cognitive, 18, 32, 98

emotional, 113-118
Conformism, 10, 32, 84, 88, 116
Conformist stage, 113-115
Congruence, 70, 81
Conjunctive Faith, stage, 108-110
Conscience, 18-20, 31, 43-44, 54-56, 63, 88-89
Conscientiousness, 72, 96
Conscientious stage, 113-115
Consciousness, 18, 35-36
Consensus, 88
Consequences, 42-43, 51, 100
Consistency, value, 67
Constitutional psychology, 78-80
Constraint, 32, 48-49
Consumerism, 106
Contemplation, 89, 117
Contextualistic pragmatism, 76
Contextual knowledge, 75
Contractual orientation, 113
Contradiction, 79, 109
Conventional values, 84
Conventional level of morality, 88-97, 115
  (*see also* Kohlberg, Lawrence)
Conventions, social, 90
Cooperation, 11, 23-25, 32-33, 48-49, 87
Conversion, 110
Coping mechanisms, 116
Coser, Rose, 48
Counseling, 79-80
Courage, 41, 75-76, 95, 105
Creation-destruction polarity, 103
Creativity, 8
Crisis, 83, 100-103
Criticalness, 78
Critical thinking, 72-75, 109
Cross-cultural differences, 6, 99
Cross-cultural studies, 59
Cross-cultural validation, 107
Cross-sectional data, 96-97
Crowd-pleaser, 71
Cruelty, 95
Cultural relativism, 87-93
Cultural tolerance, 93
Culture, 7-8, 17-19, 21-22, 45, 49-50, 54-57, 62, 80-81, 87, 92-93, 105, 117
Curiosity, 78
Curriculum, 36, 67, 98
Cynicism, 109

D

Damon, William, 89
Death, 57, 103, 108
Death instinct, 24 (*see* Thanatos)
Decentering, 49
Deception, 114
Defects, 38
Defense mechanism, 19, 44-45, 85
Defensive identification, 44-45
Deferred values, 55
Definition
  conventional, 105
  operational, 57
  stipulative, 5-6, 105
Democracy, 25-28, 88, 98, 117
Denney, R., 10
Dependence, 13, 36, 50, 70, 102, 108-109
Depth psychology, 17 (*see* Psychoanalysis)
Deprivation, 105, 108
Description, 32, 94, 105
Descriptive relativism, 92
Desired values, 55
Desires, 11, 18-19, 30
Despair, 60
Detachment, 78
Deutscher, Irwin, 16
Developing competence, 72
Developing integrity, 70
Development
  cognitive, 7
  definition, 7
  historical, 12
  intellectual, 7
  moral, 7
  social, 7
Developmental education, 36
Developmental patterns, 74-75
Developmental problems, 71
Developmental sequences, 90-91
Developmental stages, 48-49, 59-60, 88-99, 105-111
Developmental tasks, 4, 53-58, 72, 101
Developmental transitions, 102
Deviance, 9
DeVitis, Joseph L., 28-29, 32, 47, 120
Dewey, John, 87-90
Dialectics, 39-40, 109
Differentiated person-lity, 40

Diffusion of ideals, 60
Dilemma, 90, 113-114, 118
Directing of behavior, 42 (*see also* Sears, Robert R.)
Direct tuition, 44
Disappointment, 102
Disapproval, 88
Discipline, 11-12
Discrimination, 57-58
Discussion, of moral issues, 97-98
Dishonesty, 67, 89-90, 95
Disputes, verbal, 84
Dissident youth, 83-85
Distortion, 109
Distributive justice, 119
Distrust, 84
Disturbing information, 81-82
Divergent thinking, 35
Diversity, 75, 80, 93
Divorce, 102
Dogmatism, 76
Dollard, John, 42
Donaldson, Margaret, 49
Donne, John, 79
Doob, Leonard W., 42
Dostoevsky, Fyodor, 79
Doubt, 60
Drama, 99-100, 108
Dreams, 18, 101, 103
Dreikurs, Rudolf, 26-27, 29-30
Drives, 57, 81
Dualism, 40, 75-76, 89
Dualistic stage, 75
Durkheim, Emile, 4, 11-18, 27, 34, 36-37, 48, 59
Duty, 88, 117
Duty orientation, 88

E

Early Adult Transition, 100
Eastern culture, 110
Economic factors, 8, 54-55, 62
Education
  collective, 37
  college, 66-86
  content, 8
  definition, 7-8, 12
  developmental, 36
  elementary, 36

goals, 107
higher, 66-86
individual, 37-38
institutions, 8
moral, 97-98
objectives, 8, 57, 73
outcomes, 8
planning, 57
practices, 110
secondary, 55
standards, 8
system, 84
tasks, 75
through example, 37
Educators, 12, 14 (*see also* Teachers)
Effort, 75
Egalitarianism, 26-27, 48-49
Ego, 18-20, 60-61, 91, 112-116
Egocentrism, 25, 36, 43, 49, 67, 84
Ego development, 102, 112-116
Ego-ideal, 18-19, 30
Ego-identity, 61
Ego integrity, 60
Egoism, 12, 89
Ego psyhology, 59-61, 112-116
Ego stability, 112
Ego strength, 26, 82, 114
Eight Stages of Man, 59-60 (*see also* Erikson, Erik H.)
Electra complex, 20-21
Elementary education, 8 (*see also* Education)
Eliot, T.S., 79
Emerson, Ralph Waldo, 79
Emotions, 30, 55-57, 69, 95-96, 113-114, 118, 120
Empathy, 25
Empiricism, 44, 81, 96
Empty nest, 102
Encouragement, 101
Enlightened self-interest, 19, 24, 30-31, 41
Entering Adult World, 100-101
Entering Middle Adulthood, 103-104
Environment
  college, 70-71
  conditions, 7, 13, 37
  laws, 10
  nurturing, 106

school, 98
  ultimate, 105-107
Epicureanism, 7, 73
Epstein, R., 50
Equality, 48-50, 52, 88, 119-120
Era, concept, 99, 107
Erikson, Erik H., 4, 37, 53, 59-65, 91, 98-
  99, 102, 105, 107, 111
Eroticism, 19
Esprit de corps, 73
Essay writing, 79
Essentialism, 58
Establishing identity, 69, 72
Etiquette, 6
Ethical behavior, 7
Ethical consolidation, 63
Ethical differences, 119
Ethical inquiry, 7
Ethical interpretation, 44
Ethical language, 7
Ethical principles, 88-89
Ethical relativism, 90, 92
Ethical statements, 94
Ethical system, 54
Ethical terms, 104
Ethical values, 7
Ethics
  and morals, 63
  definition, 6-7
  normative, 73, 94
  systems of, 7
Ethnicity, 57, 99-100
Ethnocentrism, 71
Evaluation
  behavioral, 72-73
  moral, 93
Evil, 39-40
Example, teaching by, 89
Exceptional children, 38
Executives, business, 99
Exhortation, 64, 89
Existentialism, 76, 115-116
Expectations, social, 88, 108-109
Experience
  emotional, 51, 55, 113
  moral, 103, 111
  non-dualistic, 89
  personal, 99-100
Experiential awareness, 115

Experimental schools, 29
Experimentation, ideological, 63
Explanation, 46, 105, 111
Exploitation, 114
Exploration, 101-103
External world, 35-36, 49, 81-82

F

Facts
  psychological, 94
  social, 15
Factual statements, 94
Faculty
  accessibility, 71
  college, 73
  interaction with students, 71
Failure, 103
Fairness, 48-49, 96, 117-118
Faith
  definition, 105
  development, 5, 73, 105-111
  identity, 106-107
Fame, 106
Family, 12, 22, 26, 29-30, 54, 84, 100-
  101, 106-108, 119
Family therapy, 27
Fanaticism, 62-63, 76
Fantasy, 18, 34-37, 40-41, 44, 78-79, 84,
  108
Fear, 78, 108
Feeling, 38-39
Feldman, Kenneth A., 68, 73
Feminine experience, 111-120
Feminism, 21-23, 40, 119
Fetishism, 106
Fiction, 99-100
Fictional heroes, 42-43
Fidelity, 62
Fine arts, 80
Fixed moral rules, 87-88
Focal attention, 47-48
Food, 55
Formal education, 8
Formalism, 93
Forms, moral, 94
Fowler, James W., 5, 105-111
Fox, Seymour, 20
France, 13
Fraenkel, Jack R., 95

Frankena, William K., 92
Frankl, Viktor, 57
Fraud, 95
Freeing interpersonal relationships, 70, 72
Freud, Sigmund, 4, 16-36, 41-45, 52, 60, 111, 117 (*see also* Psychoanalysis)
Friendship, 31, 70-71, 78-79, 100, 105, 119
Frustration, 45-46, 99
Fulfillment, 99
Fully functioning human being, 78, 109-110
Functionalism, 91
Future goals, 61

G

Gallup polls, 3
Gandhi, Mahatma, 59, 64, 110
Game of marbles, 47, 50-52, 111 (*see also* Piaget, Jean)
Gehlke, Charles E., 15
Gender, roles, 21
General education, 67, 79
Generativity, 60, 102
Generations, 59, 85
Genetic epistemology, 46 (*see also* Piaget, Jean)
Genital stage, 60
Genocide, 6
Germany, 58, 64
Gilligan, Carol, 5, 21, 24, 331, 96, 112, 117-120
Glazer, Nathan, 10
Goal achievement, 69, 115
Golden Rule, 63-64, 73, 89
Good behavior, 42-43
Good boy orientation, 88, 113
Good temper, 89
Goslin, D.A., 87
Government, 98, 110
Greece, 20-21, 120
Grief, 102
Grief, Esther B., 96
Group(s)
 expectations, 88
 minority, 119
 primary, 109
 reference, 71
 social, 61

 standards, 76
Growth, 103-104
 as moral issue, 75-76
 definition, 74
Gruber, Howard E., 52
Guiding values, 82
Guilt, 18, 20, 43, 60, 95

H

Habits, 11, 14, 95
Hall, G. Stanley, 20, 34, 36
Hammarskjold, Dag, 110
Happiness, 53, 57, 84, 116
Haranguers, 71
Hard work, 75
Hartshorne, Hugh, 89-90
Harvard University, 74, 83-84, 118
Haverford College, 82-83
Head Start, 90
Health, psychological, 83
Heath, Douglas H., 5, 66, 81-86
Heath, Harriet E., 81
Heath, Roy, 5, 66, 77-81
Hedonistic orientation, 113
Hedonism, 88
Heinz case, 91, 118
Henotheistic type, 106
Heredity, 7
Heschel, Abraham, 110
Heteronomy, 9-10
Heteronomous morality, 48-49
Hierarchy
 developmental, 104
 schema, 91
 structure, 111
 value, 93
Higher education, 4, 66-86 (*see also* College)
Hinduism, 105-106
Hippies, 61
History
 as subject matter, 55
 development of, 12
 evolutionary, 25-26
 figures in, 99-100
 intellectual, 119
Hoffer, Eric, 76
Hoffman, L.W., 87, 112
Hoffman, M.L., 87, 112

Hogan, Robert, 23, 50
Holism, 106-107
Home
  authority, 9
  influence, 70
Homonomy, 10
Honduras, 90
Honesty, 72, 89-90, 95
Horney, Karen, 23
Hourly workers, 99
Household chores, 26
Hull, Clark L., 42
Human Betterment Foundation, 51
Human concern, 12, 31
Humanities, 36, 79-80
Human organization, 11-12
Human relations, courses, 68
Humor, 78
Hurting others, 31, 117
Hypothetical questions, 118

I

Identification, 42-46
  anaclitic, 44-45
  defensive, 44-45
  maternal, 84
  paternal, 85
  sex-role, 45
Id, 18
Idealism, 115-116
Ideals, diffusion of, 60
Identity, 59-61, 69-72, 109
Identity confusion, 59-61
Identity consciousness, 60-61
Identity crisis, 4, 37, 59-61
Identity polarization, 60
Ideological experimentation, 63
Ideology, 61-65, 84-86, 109
Idolatry, 106
Illness, 57, 103, 116
Illusion, 102-103
Image(s), 106-107, 111
  power, 110
  transcendent, 109-110
Imaginary figures, 99-100
Imagination, 108
Imaging, 107
Imitation, 108
Imitative phase, 108

Immanence, 48-49
Immaturity, 6
Immoral behavior, 7
Imperialism, 93
Impersonality, 93
Impulse(s), 11, 36, 78
Impulse control, 114
Impulsive stage, 113-114
Inattention, selective, 112-113
Incidental learning, 42-44
Income, 100-101
Independence, 8-13, 26, 53-54, 69, 102, 108-109
India, 90
Idiosyncracies, 38
Individual autonomy, 8-13, 19 (*see also* Autonomy)
Individual education, 37-38
Individualism, 13, 19, 23, 26, 38, 79, 117, 120
Individualism, excessive, 13
Individuality, 13, 37, 40
Individualization, 30
Individual life structure, 100
Individual moral principles, 88-89 (*see also* Principled level of morality)
Individual Psychology, 4, 29, 32 (*see also* Adler, Alfred)
Individual rights, 117
Individuation, 37
Individuative-Reflective Faith, stage, 108-109
Indoctrination, 97
Industrialism, 31
Industrial workers, 99
Industry, 60
Inequality, 29
Infancy, 6-7, 17-18, 53-55, 108, 114, (*see also* Childhood)
Infanticide, 6, 76
Infantile morality, 63
Infantile phenomena, 49-50
Inferential reference, 47-48
Inferiority, 25, 28, 60
Infidels, 6
Informal education, 8
Informal learning, 42-44
Information, disturbing, 81-82
In-group, 75

Initiative, 60
Injunctions, 20
Injustice, 57-58
Innate schema, 33, 46, 51-52
Inner-directed type, 10, 14
Inner-life activators, 78-79
Inquisition, 64
Instinct, 30-31, 35-36
Institutional change, 65
Institutionalization, of goals, 9
Institutions
  political, 85
  social, 7-8
Instructional procedures, 80 (*see also* Education)
Instrumental hedonistic stage, 88
Integrated personality, 36, 103-104
Integrated stage, 113-116
Integration, excessive, 13
Integration, self, 79
Integration, theory, 98
Integrity, 69-72, 95
Intellectual abilities, 51, 61
Intellectual activities, 84
Intellectual and ethical development, theory of, 5 (*see also* Perry, William G.)
Intellectual concepts, 54
Intellectual growth, 82
Intellectual history, 119
Intellectualization, 77-78
Intellectual purposes, 68
Intellectual skills, 54
Intelligence, 31, 51
Intelligence (IQ) testing, 51
Intentions, 50-51
Interaction, moral, 120
Interaction, of organism and environment, 7
Interdependence, 26, 70
Interdisciplinary studies, 59, 104-105
Internalization, 81-82
Internal world, 35-36, 49, 81-82
International relations, 8
Interpersonal analysis, 112 (*see also* Sullivan, Harry Stack)
Interpersonal orientation, 96
Interpersonal relationships, 25, 69, 72, 82-83, 115, 117
Interpersonal responsibility, 117

Interpersonal skills, 82
Interview techniques, 82, 96-97, 99-100, 107, 117-119
Intimacy, 60, 106
Intrapsychic phenomena, 20, 24, 30
Introjection, 37
Introspection, 78
Introversion, 14, 39
Intuition, 38-39
Intuitive-Projective Faith, stage, 108
Invariance, 46, 51, 88-93, 107, 110-111
Involvement, 78
Irrationality, 39, 52, 95-96
Isolation, 60
Israel, 90

J

Jacob, Philip E., 66-68, 86
Jacobi, Jolan, 34-35
Jacoby, Russell, 32
James, William, v
Janeway, Elizabeth, 21
Jonestown, 64
Jordan, David Starr, 51
Judgmental reasoning, 113
Judgment
  ethical, 7
  moral, 6, 91-92, 95-96
  prudential, 6
Just community, 98
Justness, 6, 95
Justice
  concept, 48-49, 89, 109-110, 115-119
  principles, 87, 91-92, 94
Justification, ethical, 7
Judaism, 63, 110
Jung, C.G., 4, 14, 20, 26, 33-40, 52, 98-99

K

Kant, Immanuel, 7, 13, 15, 73, 91, 120
Karier, Clarence J., 41, 51
Kay, William, 52
Keniston, Kenneth, 5, 66, 83-86
Kierkegaard, Sören, 79
King, Martin Luther, Jr., 64, 110
Kohlberg, Lawrence, 4-5, 16, 21, 23, 38, 46, 51, 87-98, 105-107, 110-113, 115, 117-119

Knowledge
  acquisition, 7
  contextual, 75
  requisite, 12
  transmission, 8
Kuhn, D., 97
Kurtines, William, 96

L

Labelling, 90, 98
Labor market, 62
Laing, R.D., 30
Language acquisition, 108
Lao-Tse, 4
Latency, 60, 62
Law
  education, 98
  orientation, 88, 113
  requirements, 57-58
Leadership polarization, 60
Leaders, social and political, 9
Learning
  behavioral, 7-8, 43
  conditions, 68
  incidental, 42
  informal, 42-44
  formal, 8
  moral, 63
  observational, 42
Leisure, 5, 100
Levinson, Daniel J., 5, 98-107
Liberal arts, 36, 67, 79-80
Liberal individualism, 117
Liberalism, 68, 89, 119
Libertarianism, 119
Liberty, 117
Libido, 19, 22, 61
Lickona, Thomas, 46-47, 61
Life cycle, 59-60, 99, 103, 107
Life passages, 117-118
Life, quality of, 106
Life review, 107 (*see also* Biography)
Life span development, 5, 105
Life structure, 100-103
Life style, 70, 100-101, 112
Listening, effective, 71
Literacy, political, 67
Literature, 19, 55, 79
Lloyd, Peter, 49

Locke, John, 33
Loevinger, Jane, 5, 111-117
Logic, 109
  courses, 78
Logical abilities, 51
Logical analysis, 92-93
Logical comprehensiveness, 88-89
Logical order, of development, 94-95
Logical reasoning, 92
Longitudinal studies, 68, 74, 90, 96-98, 111
Love, 5, 100-103, 108-110
Lower classes, 54-55
Loyalty, 55, 72, 106
Lukes, Steven, 15
Luther, Martin, 14, 59
Lying, 6, 48, 95

M

McGee, Reece, 9
Malevolent transformation, 114
Managing emotions, 69, 72
Mandala, 33
Manipulation, 114
Manners, 6
Marathon social sessions, 79
Maratsos, Michael, 49
Marcuse, Herbert, 22, 28-29
Marriage, 54, 100-103
Marxism, 105-106
Masculine cultural bias, 23
Masculine-feminine polarity, 103
Masculine protest, 28
Maslow, Abraham H., 109-110, 112
Mass schooling, 37
Master stories, 110
Material power, orientation, 88
Matriarchy, 45
Maturation, 7, 18, 26, 33, 35, 37, 43, 49, 57, 60-61
Mature ethics, 63
Mature relations, 53
Maturity, 81-83, 86
May, M.A., 89-90
Mead, George Herbert, 12
Meaning
  conceptual, 109
  of life, 106
Measurement instruments, 96

Media, influence, 108
Meditation, 35
Memorization, 75
Memory, 47-48
Men's moral development, 99-105, 111-120
Mental health practitioners, 3
Mental illness, 116
Mentoring, 101
Merton, Robert K., 9
Merton, Thomas, 110
Mesomorphs, 78, 80
Metaethics, 7
Meta-ethical relativism, 92
Methodological inadequacies, 105
Middle adulthood, 7, 53, 99-100
Middle Ages, 81
Middle class, 47, 54-55, 90
Mid-life Transition, 102-104, 108
Milestones of ego development, 5, 111-117
Militaristic type, 81
Mill, John Stuart, 119
Miller, Neal E., 42
Minnesota Multi-Phasic Personality Inventory (MMPI), 82
Minority groups, 119
Mistrust, 60
Modeling, 42-46, 52
Modgil, C., 96
Modgil, S., 96
Mohammed, 14
Monotheism, 106
Mood swings, 79
Moral accountability, 3, 16
Moral action, 6-7, 94-96
Moral actualization, 33, 40, 109-110
Moral behavior, 97-98
Moral categories, 93
Moral censorship, 20
Moral concepts, 6-7, 93
Moral courage, 95
Moral development, 7, 46-54, 71-86, 93, 116-117
Moral dilemma, 90
Moral diversity, 93
Moral education, 7, 63, 87-88, 97-98
Moral evaluation, 93
Moral forms, 94

Moralism, 63-64
Morality
  formal characteristics, 6, 93
  of character traits, 95
  principled, 95
Moral judgment, 91-92, 95-96
Moral language, 31
Moral logic, 14-15
Moral majority, 3
Moral participation, 49-50
Moral philosophy, 94
Moral principles, 6, 91-93
Moral realism, 48-49
Moral reasoning, 111, 118
Moral rules, 12, 87-88, 108
Morals and ethics
  distinction in, 6-7, 63
  evolution of, 62-63
Moral sensibility, 6
Moral support, 101
Moral systems, 19-20
Moral thema, 117
Moratorium, 62
Mores, 6
Moses, 14
Mother archetype, 33, 35
Mother-identification, 84
Mother Teresa, 110
Motivation, 27, 57, 83, 96
Mowrer, O.H., 42
Multidisciplinary studies, 98
Murphy, J.M., 118
Muscular physique, 78, 80
Mussen, P.H., 97
Mutuality, 88, 115-116
Myers-Briggs inventory, 39
Mysticism, 34
Mythic-Literal Faith, stage, 108
Mythology, 20-21, 108

N

Naive hedonistic orientation, 88, 113
Narcissism, 30
Nationalism, 12, 54, 64
Natural and logical consequences, 27-28
Natural man, 81
Naturalistic fallacy, 32, 64, 94, 104
Nazism, 37, 57-58, 61
Need(s)

approach, 57
domination, 81-82
of others, 96, 103
Negative identity, 60-61
Negative modeling, 42-43
Negativism, 114
Neo-analytic psychology, 34, 40 (*see also*
  Jung, C.G.)
Neurosis, 18, 25, 85
Neutralism, value, 93
Newcomb, Theodore M., 68, 73
New Testament, 110
Newton, Sir Isaac, 22
New York, 99
Niebuhr, H. Richard, 106
Nietzsche, Friedrich W., 25
Nihilism, 107
Nisbet, Robert, 15
Non-alienated youth, 84
Non-committers, 77-80
Nondirective counseling, 80
Non-dualistic experience, 89
Non-egoistic experience, 89
Nonethical terms, 104
Nonmoral conduct, 6
Nontheism, 106
Nonviolence, 109-110
Normalcy, 26
Normative analysis, v, 94, 104
Normative consensus, 9
Normative ethics, 7, 73, 94
Normative relativism, 92
Normlessness, 9, 13
Norms, 9, 10-12, 39, 52, 83
Novelists, 99
Novice phase, 100-102
Nuclear family, 30, 46

O

Obedience, 113
  orientation, 88
Obligation, 88
Objectives
  educational, 8, 57, 73
  institutional, 73
Observances, community, 108
Observational learning, 42
Observational techniques, 46, 52
Occupation, 100-103

groups, 99
preparation, 54
roles, 84
Oedipal complex, 20-21, 45
Old Testament, 110
Ontogeny, 34
Openness, 103
Operational definition, 57
Opportunism, 114
Opposites, unifying, 40, 109
Oppression, 29, 41
Oral stage, 60
Organism, 7
Organization, human, 11-12
Organizing center, 106
Oriental culture, 35
Orientation
  authority, 88, 113
  duty, 88, 113
  good boy, 88
  law, 88, 113
  material power, 88
  naive instrumental hedonistic, 88
  obedience, 88, 113
  order, 113
  physical power, 88
  punishment, 88, 113
Outer-directed type, 10, 14
Out-group, 75
Outsider, 84

P

Pain, 57
Pampering, 26, 41
Papanek, Ernst, 29
Paradox, 109, 115-116
Paranoia, 30
Parents, 7, 9, 36-37, 42-45, 48-49, 53, 85,
  101-102, 105
Participation, 49-50, 98
Passages, life, 117-118
Passion, 11
Pateman, Carole, 117
Pathology, 30
Patriarchy, 30, 45
Patricide, 20-21
Patriotism, 23, 54-55
Patterns, behavioral, 96
Peck, Robert F., 56, 112

Peers, 42-43, 48-50, 53-55, 62, 79, 101, 108-109
Pedagogy, 12, 37, (*see also* Education)
Penis envy, 21
Perceived-Self questionnaire, 82
Perceptual factors, 51
Perennialism, 58
Permissiveness, 27-28
Perry, William G., 5, 66, 74-77
Personal experiences, 99-100
Personality
  definition, 17
  mature, 49-50
  traits, 90
  typologies, 5
Personal relations, 119
Personal values, 88
Perspective-taking, 49, 108
Pessimism, 84
Peters, R.S., 95
Philosophical explanation, 87, 92
Philosophical studies of morality, 6-7
Philosophical theories of morality, 87-88
Philosophy, 79, 94
  as subject matter, 55
  courses, 98
  moral, 94-97
  of moral education, 87-88
  political, 85
Phylogeny, 20, 34
Physical activity, 55
Physical development, 53-55, 57, 69, 78
Physical power, orientation, 88
Physiological development, 61
Physiological drive, 55
Piaget, Jean, 4, 16, 27, 36, 46-52, 87, 91, 96, 98, 105, 107, 111-112
Planning, educational, 57
Plato, 34, 89
Play, 44, 62
Plungers, 77-79
Pluralism, 74, 117
Polarities, midlife, 103
Political activities, 105
Political activism, 84
Political institutions, 85
Political philosophies, 85 (*see also* Ideology)
Political literacy, 67
Polytheistic type, 106

Popular crises, 3
Population shifts, 9
Positive modeling, 42-43
Poster, Mark, 30, 32
Postconventional level of morality, 88-89, 92-96 (*see also* Kohlberg, Lawrence)
Post-modern youth, 85
Poverty, 57
Power, 17, 25, 106, 110
Powerlessness, 25
Practices, social, 15
Practice, role, 44
Practice, teaching by, 89
Pragmatism, 76
Prakash, Madhu Suri, 15, 119
Preconventional level of morality, 88-89, 92 (*see also* Kohlberg, Lawrence)
Prediction, 90, 118
Preemptiveness, 93
Prejudice, 57-58, 63, 115-116
Premoral position, 63
Prescription, 32, 58, 64
Presocial stage, 113-114
Pride, 89
Primal-horde parable, 20-21
Primary group, 109
Primary thought process, 18-19
Princeton University, 77, 80
Principled level of morality, 88-89, 95, 113 (*see also* Kohlberg, Lawrence)
Principled orientation, 113
Prinicple, of justice, 94
Principles, ethical, 88-89
Principles, moral, 91-95
Private logic, 29
Privatism, 31, 119
Problem solving, 69, 88
Procedural rules, 88
Professional-vocational curricula, 67
Professors, 71, 73 (*see also* Higher Education)
Progressivism, 58
Prohibitions, 18, 20
Projective testing, 82, 113
Property rights, 118
Prose, 79
Provocative playfulness, 62
Pseudo-self, 79
Psychoanalysis, 4, 15-31, 42-43, 47-48,

52, 92, 112-113 (*see also* Freud, Sigmund)
Psychological analysis, 94
Psychologicl awareness, 115
Psychological description, 94
Psychological facts, 94
Psychological health, 83
Psychological theory, 87, 92
Psychometrics, 113
Psychosexual development, 17, 59-60, 116
Psychosocial theory, 59 (*see also* Erikson, Erik H.)
Psychosis, 18
Psychotherapy, 17, 29, 107
Public heroes, 42-43, 46, 61
Punishment, 42-43, 48, 88, 113-114
Punishment, orientation, 88
Purpel, David, 95
Purpose
  development of, 69-71
  life, 106

Q

Quality, of life, 106

R

Race, 99, 107
Radcliffe College, 118
Random sample, 110
Radicalism, 85
Radical monotheistic type, 106
Radical youth, 5, 84-85
Rater bias, 96
Rationality, 13, 18-19, 22, 27, 35, 52, 91-93, 119-120
Rationalization, 85
Rawls, John, 119
Reality testing, 26
Realization of the Dream, 101-103
Reasonable adventurers, 77-80
Reasoning
  judgmental, 113
  logical, 92
  moral, 118
Rebellion, 26
Reciprocity, 48-49, 108
Recreation, 70
Red-diaper baby, 85 (*see also* Radical

youth)
Reductionism, 15, 24, 72
Reese, W.L., 105
Reference group, 71
Reference, inferential, 47-48
Reflective abilities, 7-8, 12, 109, 115
Reform, social, 8, 29
Relatedness, 106, 118
Relativism, 15, 74-76, 81, 87, 93, 109
  cultural, 93
  descriptive, 92
  ethical, 90, 92
  meta-ethical, 92
  sociological, 93
Religion, 19-20, 33, 54, 56, 59, 63-64, 70, 73, 99, 101, 105-111
Reliability, 72
Remarriage, 102
Renaissance, 81
Repression, 91, 28-29, 31, 45-46
Reprimand, 7
Resentment, 84
Residential community, 71 (*see also* College)
Rest, James R., 96-97
Respect, 88, 109-110, 115
Responsibility, 31, 75-76, 98, 117-119
Restraint, 18-19
Reward, 18-19, 42-43
Rich, John Martin, 12, 95-96
Rieff, Philip, 30-31
Riesman, David, 10, 14
Rigidity, 79
Right behavior, 88
Right conduct, 6-7
Righteousness, 63
Rightness, 88-89
Rights
  children's, 97
  individual, 117
  property, 118
Ritualization, 62-63
Rituals, 54
Roazen, Paul, 64-65
Rogers, Carl R., 10-11, 33, 109-110
Role diffusion, 60
Role experimentation, 60
Role playing, 78, 97

Role practice, 44
Role(s)
 cultural, 92
 family, 84
 learning, 8
 occupational, 84
 social, 52, 83, 108-109, 119
Romanticism, 61, 81
Roommates, 71 (*see also* College)
Rorschach Test, 82
Rosen, Hugh, 50
Rousseau, Jean-Jacques, 49, 117
Rule application, 50, 52
Rule making, 97
Rules
 accepting, 95
 classroom, 45, 98
 conduct, 38
 moral, 12, 87-88, 108
 obeying, 88
 procedural, 88
 rejecting, 95
 school, 98
 social, 8, 12
Russia, 58
Ryan, Kevin, 95
Ryan, William, 23, 32

S

Sample, 99
 bias, 47, 105
 nonrepresentative, 118-119
 random, 110
Sampson, Edward E., 32
Satisfactoriness, 104
Satisfying consequences, 42
Schachtel, Ernest, 47-48
Schaie, K.W., 91
Schemata, 82
School, 7, 58, 89
 authority, 9
 duties, 26
 environment, 98
 influence, 108
 role, 36
 rules, 94
Science, 94
 as subject matter, 55
 of morality, 15

Scientific investigation, 13
Scientific studies of morality, 6-7
Scientific terminology, 92-93
Scientific thinking, 93
Sears, Robert R., 4, 42-46
Seasons of a man's life, 5, 98-105 (*see also* Levinson, Daniel J.)
Secondary schools, 55 (*see also* Education)
Secondary thought process, 18
Security, 5
Selective inattention, 112-113
Self, 84, 91, 103
 actualization, 33, 40-41, 109-112
 assertiveness, 114
 certainty, 60, 109
 concept, 82, 99
 confrontation, 86
 control, 19, 43, 72, 95, 114
 derogation, 43
 determination, 11, 37, 115
 development, 117-118
 discipline, 90
 evaluation, 10-11
 examination, 86
 fulfillment, 115
 government, 9
 identity, 109
 insight, 29
 instruction, 43-44
 integration, 79
 justification, 106
 knowledge, 82
 mastery, 114
 organization, 81
 perception, 56-57
 respect, 79
 system, 112-113
 understanding, 101
Selfishness, 108
Self-image questionnaire, 82
Self-protective stage, 113-114
Self, sense of, 106
Senior thesis, 79
Sensation, 38-39
Sensibility, 6
Sensitive-to-the-rule type, 14
Sensitivity, 96, 115
Sentence-completion testing, 113-116
Sequence, of moral development, 93

Serow, Robert C., 120
Settling Down, 100-102
Sex
  awareness, 108
  differentiation, 21, 28, 99
  education, 98
  instincts, 19, 24
  roles, 45, 53
Sexual equality, 28, 119
Sexual identification, 45
Sexual identity, 60
Sexuality, 17-18, 106-107
Sexual stereotyping, 45
Shadow figure, 39-40
Shame, 43, 60
Sheldon, William H., 80
Sichel, Betty A., v, 31, 117
Simmel, Georg, 22-23
Simpson, Elizabeth L., 95
Singer, June, 40
Sizer, Nancy F., 89
Sizer, Theodore R., 89
Skills
  acquisition, 7
  concept, 82
Skinner, b.F., 42, 46
Slavery, 6, 119
Social attachment, 11-13
Social change, 12, 29, 65, 85
Social class, 54-57, 99-101
Social community, 31 (*see also* Community)
Social contract orientation, 88
Social control, 9
Social conventions, 90
Social deprivation, 105
Social disorganization theory, 8-9
Social equality, 23, 26-27, 119
Social expectations, 57, 88, 108-109
Social experience, 48-49
Social facts, 15
Social feelings, 20, 26 (*see also* Community)
Social forces, 18, 24
Social groups, 11-12, 61
Social ideals, 23
Social interaction, 120
Social interest, 14, 24-26 (*see also* Adler, Alfred)
Socialization, 7-9, 12, 21, 45-46, 57, 67-68, 84-85

Social learning, 42, 44-48, 52
Social logic, 14-15
Social milieu theory, 12
Social order, 27, 88
Social practices, 15
Social reality, 14, 81-82
Social relationships, 24, 100-102, 106, 119
Social roles, 5, 83, 108-109, 119
Social rules, 12
Social science methodologies, 6-7
Social service, 54-55
Social skills, 82
Social stability, 4, 8-13, 27, 33
Social standards, 32
Social studies, 98
Social system, 9
Sociobiology, 33
Socio-cultural synthesis, 4 (*see also* Erikson, Erik H.)
Sociological relativism, 93
Sociology of knowledge, 16
Socrates, 14
Solidarity, 13
Solitude, 78
Soltz, Vicki, 26-27
Somatype, 80
Soviet Union, 58, 81
Spartans, 81
Specific behavior, 89-90
Species-specific behavior, 7
Spoiling, 41, (*see also* Pampering)
Stability, 103
Stage(s)
  definition, 90-91
  developmental, 100-111
  theories, 48-49, 88-92, 100-111
Stagnation, 60, 102
Stalinism, 58
Standardization, 96
Standards
  community, 26, 32,57
  group, 26, 32, 57-58
Stanford University, 51
Stereotyping, sex-role, 45
Stipulative definition, 6, 105
Stoicism, 7, 73, 120
Stories, 108-110
Story-telling techniques, 47, 50-52, 111 (*see also* Piaget, Jean)

Stress, 95
Striving for power, 92-93
Strivings for superiority, 25, 28
Structuralism, 46-47, 87-97, 107, 111 (*see also* Cognitive-Structuralism)
Students(s), 14
  and faculty, 71
  radicals, 5, 84-85
  values, 66-86
Subcultures, 101
Subjectivity, 39, 48-49, 59, 117-118
Sublimation, 19
Success, 53, 103, 106
Suffering, 109-110
Suicidal types, 13
Sullivan, Harry Stack, 112, 114
Superego, 18-19, 45, 61
Support system, 70-71, 101
Suppression, 109
Surplus repression, 28-29
Symbiotic stage, 113-114
Symbolization, 81-83, 103, 108-109
Sympathy, 31
Synthetic-Conventioonal Faith, stage, 108-110
Szasz, Thomas, 52

T

Tabula rasa, 33
Taiwan, 90
Tasks
  developmental, 4, 53-58, 72, 101
  educational, 75, 107
Taste, 6
Teachers, 20, 57, 79, 97-98 (*see also* Education)
  authority, 9
  methods, 68, 79-80
  quality, 67-68
  role, 36
Technology, 8, 83
Temperance, 89
Ten Commandments, 89
Teresa, Mother, 110
Terman, Lewis M., 42, 51
Thanatos, 24 (*see also* Death instinct)
Theism, 105-106
Thematic Apperception Test (TAT), 83-84, 99-100
Theology, 106, 111

Theory, 87, 92
  definition, 7
  integration, 98
  moral development, 7
  social disorganization, 8-9
Therapy, 17, 29, 107
Thesis, senior, 79
Time diffusion, 60
Time perspective, 60
Thinking
  critical, 73, 75
  divergent, 35
  patterns, 38-39, 108
  scientific, 93
  stimulation of, 88-89
Tolerance, 5, 68, 71, 78, 93, 120
Toronto, 107
Totalism, 62-63
Total person, 41, 72
Tradition, 8
Tradition-directed type, 10
Transitions, developmental, 102
Transmission, knowledge, 8
Transcendence, 106-110
Trauma, 84
Trial and error, 44
Tribalism, 106
Trust, 60, 106-108
Truthfulness, 6-7, 89
Turiel, E., 97
Turkey, 89-90
Typologies
  personality, 77-81
  schema, 59-60
  theory, 38-39
Tyrant, 71

U

Ultimate concern, 106-107
Ultimate reality, 105
Uncertainty, 75-76
Uncommitted youth, 5, 83-85
Unconscious, 17-19, 35, 39, 109
  collective, 34
  personal, 34
Undifferentiated Faith, stage, 108
Unhappiness, 57
United States, 20, 81, 84
Universalism, 63-64, 106
Universality, 88-89, 91, 93

moral forms, 94
moral paradigms, 5, 17, 30, 46
moral patterns, 87-88, 99, 105-107, 110-111
moral principles, 15
Universalizing Faith, stage, 108-110
University biologists, 99
Utilitarianism, 7, 73
Utility values, 73
Upper-class, 54-55
  youth, 118
Utopianism, 59, 65

V

Validity, empirical, 96
Valuators, 82
Value(s)
  analysis and appraisal, 72
  center, 110
  concept, 54, 71, 100-102, 106-109, 115
  consistency, 67
  core, 85
  deferred, 55
  definition, 72-73
  desired, 55
  exploration, 86
  formation, 55
  guiding, 82
  hierarchy, 93
  identification, 21
  internalization, 21
  neutralism, 93
  patterns, 72
  personal, 88
  relativism, 93
  role, 73
  set, 56
  social, 56
  standards, 72-73
  statements, 72-73
  systems, 62-64, 70
  transcendent, 106
  utility, 73
Value-upholding process, 97-98
Vectors of Development, 5, 69-72 (*see also* Chickering, Arthur W.)
Verbal disputes, 84
Verbal facility, 97
Victorian society, 17, 30
Vietnam, 46

Vietnam Summer, 84-85
Vices, 87-95
Virgin, 33
Virtues, 6, 87, 89-90, 95
Vocational plans, 70
Vocational-professional curricula, 67
Vonèche, J. Jacques, 52
Vonnegut, Kurt, Jr., 31

W

Warmth, 55
Watergate, 46
Way, Lewis, 29
Wealth, 81, 106
Weber, Max, 14
Well-being, psychological, 116
Wellwork, Ernest, 13
Wessler, Ruth, 113, 117
Western culture, 13, 58, 117
White imperialism, 93
Whole person, 58
Will, 75
Will to power, 25
Wilson, Edward O., 33
Williams, N., 94
Williams, S., 94
Withdrawal, 109
Withey, S.B., 86
Wittgenstein, Ludwig, 76
Wolff, Robert Paul, 119
Wolman, Benjamin B., 96
Women's causes, 119
Women's moral development, 5, 17, 20-23, 96, 111-120
Work, 5, 60, 62, 75, 90, 99, 103
Workaholism, 106
Wright, J. Eugene, Jr., 65
Writing, essay, 79

Y

Young adulthood, 108-109
Youth
  affluent, 85
  alienated, 83-86
  culture, 84
  dissident, 83-86
  post-modern, 85
  radical, 84-86
  uncommitted, 83-84
Yucatan, 90